Echoes of Devotion

The Mahāns of Mahārāshtra

Subi Subramanian

OrangeBooks Publication

1st Floor, Rajhans Arcade, Mall Road, Kohka, Bhilai, Chhattisgarh 490020

Website: **www.orangebooks.in**

First Edition, 2025

ISBN: 978-93-6554-400-8

Price: Rs. 430.00

Printed in India

ECHOES OF DEVOTION

THE MAHĀNS OF MAHĀRĀSHTRA

A SPIRITUAL ODYSSEY THROUGH TIME AND TRADITION

SUBI SUBRAMANIAN

OrangeBooks Publication
www.orangebooks.in

This book is dedicated to the Mahāns of Mahārāshtra

who inspired me right from my childhood in Pune, Mahārāshtra, India and taught me the value of humility and devotion.

~ ***Subi Subramanian***

Blessings from Swami Govindadev Giri Maharaj

The author is deeply blessed and honored to receive a message of benediction from Revered Swami Govindadev Giri Maharaj for this book.

Swamiji is a renowned Indian spiritual Guru whose life and work continue to inspire countless seekers. As the Treasurer of the Shri Ram Janmabhoomi Teerth Kshetra Trust—responsible for the construction of the sacred Shri Ram Janmabhoomi Temple in Ayodhya—and the Vice President of the Krishna Janmabhoomi Trust in Mathura, Swamiji plays a pivotal role in preserving and nurturing the spiritual and cultural heritage of Bharat.

His contributions extend deeply into the world of spiritual education through institutions such as the Sant Dnyaneshwar Gurukul, which he founded in Alandi, Maharashtra at the same place sanctified by the presence of Sant Dnyaneshwar Maharaj.

An ardent devotee of Sant Dnyaneshwar, Swamiji has made the teachings of the Shri Dnyaneshwari—the Marathi rendering of the Srimad Bhagavad Gita—the compass of his spiritual life.

To have Swamiji's blessings for this humble work is an immense privilege. The author offers humble pranams and heartfelt gratitude at Swamiji's holy feet and prays for his continued grace and guidance.

स्वामी गोविन्ददेव गिरि

आचार्य- डी.लिट्. (मानद)

उपाध्यक्ष, श्रीकृष्ण जन्मभूमि ट्रस्ट, मथुरा

कोषाध्यक्ष, श्रीरामजन्मभूमि तीर्थक्षेत्र (न्यास), अयोध्या

॥ श्रीहरिः ॥

'धर्मश्री', सूर्यमुखी दत्तमंदिर के समीप,

पुणे विद्यापीठ मार्ग, पुणे ४११०१६

दूरभाष : (०२०) २५६५२५८९

फॅक्स : (०२०) २५६७२०६९

swamigovindgiriji@gmail.com

Benediction

Our country is indeed fortunate to be blessed by the Almighty with the reassuring promise that He Himself will reincarnate in this land periodically when the evil forces run amok. And truly, besides the famous ten Avataras, we have witnessed numerous Vibhutis that manifested themselves here cutting across boundaries of time, region, castes or gender.

The same is true of Maharashtra where we find an abundance of Sant's beginning with the Middle Ages. They spread the message of God in the lingua franca Marathi, opened the pathway to God to everyone in the form of Bhakti (supreme Love for God) and Naamjapa (Chanting the name of God). In the darkest night of the demonic rule of evil external powers, they provided motherly moral support to the people and maintained their morale. Elsewhere in the world, in the absence of such support, we find whole countries overrun by cultural devastation.

Unfortunately, this unique service of the Sants hasn't received its full share of appreciation outside Maharashtra. One of the reasons is the non-availability of their literature, rich with literary and philosophical treasure, in other languages, including English.

Nowadays though, this picture is slowly changing. Shri. Sundaresan Subramanian's 'Echoes of Devotion' is the latest and most commendable attempt in this direction. I am sure that his prolonged stay and exposure to the Marathi ethos gives his book more authenticity than any other 'outsider' dependent on translations.

I am sure that 'Echoes of Devotion' will prove to be an opening door to the spiritual tradition of Maharashtra.

I pray to the Almighty that more such books flow from the pen of the author.

In the service of Bharatmata

स्वामी गोविंददेवगिरि

(Swami Govindadev Giri)

। महर्षि वेदव्यास प्रतिष्ठान । गीता परिवार । संत श्री ज्ञानेश्वर गुरुकुल । श्रीकृष्ण सेवा निधि ।

Email : dharmashree123@gmail.com | Website : www.dharmashree.org

Vithoba or Vittal is a form of Lord Vishnu
worshipped at Pandharpur in Mahārāshtra, India
Photo Source: Creative Commons CC0 License

Varkaris (devotees of Vithoba) sing and dance with joy at the Palki festival.

Photo Source: Creative Commons CC0 License

Prominent Mahāns of Mahārāshtra

Sant Dnyaneshwar

Sant Namdeo

Sant Eknath

Sant Tukaram

Sant Ramdas

Sant Chokhamela

About the Book

The Sanskrit word 'Mahān translates to "great," "magnificent," or "noble."

It is often used to describe someone possessing greatness, nobility, or grandeur in various contexts, whether moral, spiritual, or social. In this book, the author uses "Mahān" to refer to a saint, as it aligns with the traditional reverence the term conveys. Throughout the book, the author uses both "Mahān" and "Saint" interchangeably to convey the same meaning. Likewise, the names Vittal and Vithoba refer to the same deity and mean the same.

Mother India has given birth to numerous Mahāns who worshipped the Supreme power out of implicit devotion alone. Among them many were born in the state of Mahārāshtra, which means "great state."

In the vibrant tapestry of Mahārāshtra's cultural and spiritual heritage, the Mahāns of the region stand as enduring symbols of devotion, wisdom, and moral strength. This book, "Echoes of Devotion: The Mahāns of Mahārāshtra," is a tribute to these remarkable figures whose lives and teachings have shaped the spiritual landscape of the state.

"Echoes of Devotion" delves into the lives of Mahārāshtra's revered saints, from the profound philosophical musings of Sant Dnyaneshwar to the heartfelt devotional hymns of Sant Tukaram. Each chapter is a journey through their sacred teachings, exploring how their messages of love, humility, and spirituality transcended time and continue to resonate with people today.

This book explores the lives and teachings of some of the spiritual giants of Mahārāshtra. The saints of Mahārāshtra emphasized devotion to God, the importance of humility, and the rejection of caste distinctions. Their accomplishments and devotional hymns have left an indelible mark on the Sant tradition and continue to inspire spiritual seekers.

In this book, we have briefly covered each prominent saint's contributions to spirituality, literature, and social reform.

Beyond just recounting their lives of such saints, this book seeks to contextualize their teachings in today's world, reflecting on their relevance in contemporary society.

Through meticulous research, evocative narratives, and deep reflections, this book aims to offer readers a comprehensive understanding of these saintly figures and their profound impact not only on Mahārāshtra's spiritual and cultural identity but also on the global community.

In celebrating the saints of Mahārāshtra, the author invites readers to explore the broader spiritual legacy of the region, encouraging a deeper connection with the timeless wisdom that these saints imparted. It is a journey into the heart of Mahārāshtra's devotional history, one that will resonate with scholars, spiritual seekers, philosophers and anyone interested in the rich tapestry of Indian spiritual traditions.

The Abhangs, or devotional songs of these great saints in Marathi, have transcended the borders of Mahārāshtra, reaching audiences around the globe. Today, they form an integral part of the 'Sampradaya Bhajan' tradition that was initiated much later by the saints in South India. The legacy of Mahārāshtra's Mahāns endures, as they crafted this simple yet profound method of self-purification and worship.

The author had the opportunity and privilege to visit many of the holy places in Mahārāshtra including Pandharpur, Alandi, Dehu, Shirdi, and Hadshi. The book shares many of the photos taken by him at these places.

Echoes of Devotion: Mahāns of Mahārāshtra is more than just a historical account; it is a celebration of the enduring power of unwavering faith and the transformative influence of spiritual leadership, which paves the way for a new path for future generations.

About the Author

Sundaresan ("Subi") Subramanian is a distinguished professional in energy and environmental management, with a career that spans over five decades in multinational corporations and U.S. government agencies. His extensive international experience is bolstered by impressive academic credentials and training in engineering and management from India, UK, Japan and the USA.

Raised in Pune, the cultural heart of Mahārāshtra, Subi developed a profound connection to the region's spiritual traditions from an early age. As a school student, he was captivated by the annual Pandharpur Yatra, where thousands of devotees, known as "Varkari," walk approximately 250 kilometers from Alandi and Dehu to Pandharpur, a pilgrim city with a temple of Pandurang considered an incarnation of Lord Vishnu. The Varkari pilgrims carry palkhis (palanquins) with the holy padukas (footwear) of saints, singing devotional songs throughout the journey. The vibrant celebrations and the collective spirit of the procession left a lasting impression on him, inspiring him to explore the lives of these saints and their significant impact on the community.

Throughout his career and personal life — marked by his participation in numerous bhajans and discourses in the U.S. and India — Subi has been deeply moved by the powerful yet simple stories of these saints who were ordinary people but spiritual giants who earned enduring reverence without holding any positions of power. Subi loved and learnt some of the 'Abhangs' – a form of devotional poetry in Marathi language sung in praise of the Hindu god Vittal- that form an essential part of Sampradaya bhajans. This book reflects the inspiration he has drawn from the Maharashtrian saints and their devotional compositions. It aims to offer readers insights into the lives of these revered figures and to share the wisdom and spiritual guidance that have enriched his own life. The author hopes this book will not only deepen readers' understanding of the saints of Mahārāshtra but also inspire them to embrace the lessons of devotion and humility for a more fulfilling life.

Contents

Chapter - 1
About Mahārāshtra, India 1

Chapter - 2
The Glory Of Pandharpur 6

Chapter - 3
Prominent Mahāns Of Mahārāshtra 10

Chapter - 4
The Bhakti Movement 13

Chapter - 5
The Role Of Mahārāshtrian Mahāns 17

Chapter - 6
Sant Dnyaneshwar 21

Chapter - 7
Sant Eknath 31

Chapter - 8
Sant Namdev 36

Chapter - 9
Sant Tukaram 41

Chapter - 10
Sant Ramdas 49

Chapter - 11
Sant Chokhamela 59

Chapter - 12

Sant Gora Kumbhar 62

Chapter - 13

Women Saints Of Mahārāshtra 64

Chapter - 14

Marathi Abhangs 68

Chapter - 15

The Varkari Tradition 79

Chapter - 16

Reverence For Saints 84

Chapter - 17

The Echoes Of Devotion 87

Chapter - 18

The Modern-Era Mahāns 92

Chapter - 19

Key Lessons 101

Chapter - 20

Holy Places 103

Chapter - 21

Resources For Information 107

Chapter - 22

Reference Books 109

Other Publications of the Author 111

Chapter - 1

About Mahārāshtra, India

Mahārāshtra in Marathi literally means Mahā - Great, Rashtra-State, A Great State!

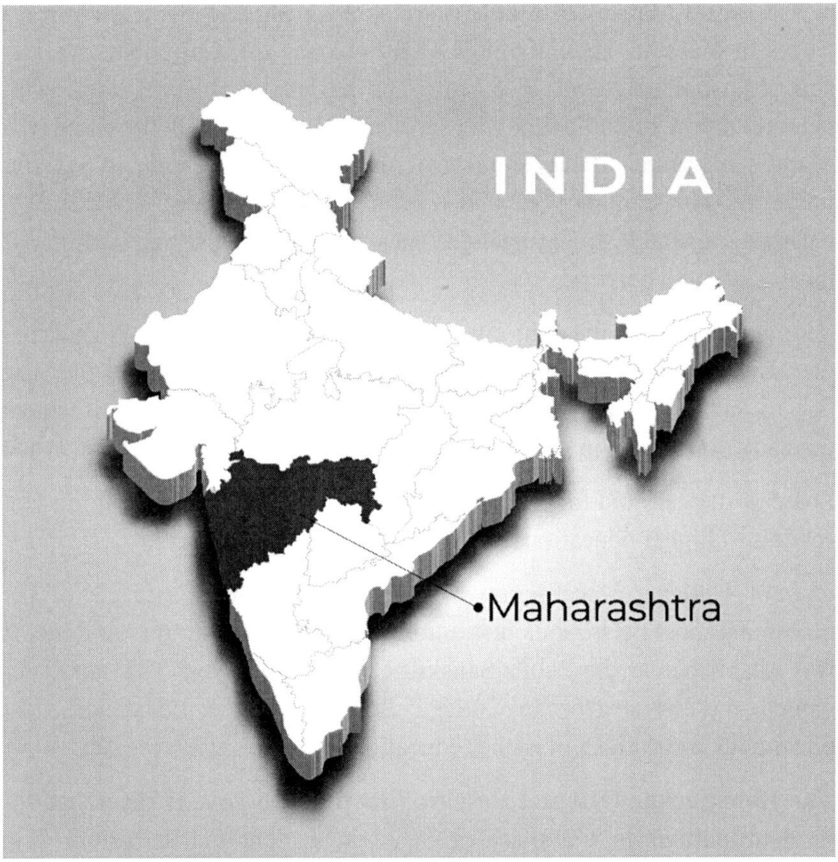

Mahārāshtra, a beautiful state in western India, is known for its rich cultural and ecological heritage. The state is renowned for its scenic Western Ghats and diverse ecosystems. The state is home to many historical landmarks, including the Ajanta and Ellora Caves, which are UNESCO World Heritage Sites. These ancient rock-cut caves are renowned for their intricate sculptures and paintings. Additionally, the forts of Mahārāshtra, like Simhagad and Raigad, are historically significant.

It has been home to many historical figures such as the Maratha warrior King Chatrapati Shivaji Maharaj, the freedom fighter Bal Gangadhar Tilak, and Dr. Babasaheb Ambedkar, the architect of the Indian Constitution.

Marathi is an ancient and popular language of Mahārāshtra. To reach the masses, most Mahāns of Mahārāshtra spoke, sang and wrote significant works in Marathi. Their writings often took the form of poems, verses, and philosophical texts. The state has a rich literary tradition, with numerous writers and poets who have made significant contributions to Marathi literature. Mahārāshtra has contributed significantly to Marathi literature, with famous poets and writers like Vishnu Shastri Chiplunkar, Kusumagraj, and P. L. Deshpande. The state also has a strong tradition of theater, art, and cinema.

Pune is considered the best city on the Deccan Plateau. So, it acquired the name of Queen of Deccan. Pune is called as the Oxford of the East due to having the greater number of educational institutes and centers than any other place in India.

Some of the very old institutions in Pune include the following important schools of higher education:

Deccan College, a well-known school of languages, and one of the oldest and most prestigious institutions of higher education is in Pune. It was established as the Poona Sanskrit College in the year 1821 and later named in 1864 as Deccan College. It is one of the oldest and most prestigious institutions of higher education in Pune.

The Bhandarkar Oriental Research Institute in Pune is renowned for its contributions to the study of Sanskrit, ancient Indian history, and various aspects of Indian culture and languages.

Vibrant Community

The Author with Vasudev

Mahārāshtra is home to a vibrant community that includes a wide range of ethnic groups, languages, and traditions. It has a long and proud tradition of song, dance, music and theatre. The people of Mahārāshtra are generally simple, outspoken and religiously inclined. There are numerous small and big temples dotting the entire state. The state is known for its vibrant festivals like Ganesh Chaturthi, Gudi Padwa, and Diwali. It is also famous for its classical dance forms such as Lavani and Tamasha. The state has a deep spiritual and religious history that attracts devotional people from all over the world.

In Mahārāshtra, there is a wandering nomadic tribe known as 'Vasudev' known for their dedication to singing bhakti songs (devotional hymns) that pay homage to Lord Krishna (Son of Vasudeva).

A typical street song by the 'Vasudev' sounds more like a Bhajan in the glory of Lord Krishna. It is something like...

Govind Rama Ho, Gopala Rama Ji-Ji

Keshava Rama Ho, Madhava Rama Ji-Ji

The Vasudevs live primarily on the voluntary alms given by others, rarely asking for money, but graciously accepting into a bag whatever is offered voluntarily. Their unwavering devotion to bhakti singing is truly admirable.

For five consecutive centuries, Mahārāshtra was blessed with the appearance of incomparable saints, particularly during the 13th and 14th centuries. They were all devotees of Shri Vittal, also known as Panduranga (an incarnation of Vishnu), whose temple is situated in the holy town of Pandharpur on the banks of the Chandrabhaga River.

What made them so wonderful? It is the beautiful poetry of divine love with which they expressed their deep longing and joy and the unity that bound them all in the love of God. Their songs still reflect the holy thoughts of yore, as they are sung not only in every town and village of Mahārāshtra but in many places around the globe.

Saints of Mahārāshtra

Among the notable saints of Mahārāshtra are Sants Dnyaneshwar, Namdev, Tukaram, Ekanath, and Ramdas who played key roles in the Bhakti movement.

There were many notable women saints of Mahārāshtra including the following:

Saint Sakhubai: She was a 12th-century saint who lived in Pandharpur. Sakhubai's deep faith and devotion to Lord Vittal were legendary, and she is revered as a symbol of unwavering devotion.

Saint Muktabai: She was a 13th-century saint and the younger sister of the prominent saint and poet, Saint Dnyaneshwar.

Saint Janabai: She was a 13th-century saint and a devotee of Lord Vittal. Janabai's compositions, known as "Abhangs," express her unwavering love and devotion to God.

Saint Bahinabai: She was a Marathi poet and saint who lived in the 17th century. Her poetry reflects her devotion to God and her deep spiritual experiences.

Saint Soyarabai: She was a 17th-century saint and the wife of Sant Tukaram. Soyarabai supported Tukaram in his spiritual pursuits and composed many songs.

Thus, the Marathi community, characterized by its rich traditions and enviable history of saints has made significant contributions to Indian culture and society.

Bhakti knows no bounds and Mahārāshtra is a forerunner in the matter of cultivating Bhajans and Bhakti in both the simplest ways.

In this book, we focus on some of the most influential saints, or 'Mahāns,' from Mahārāshtra who transformed the state's cultural identity with the practice of Bhakti or devotion through their speeches, writings and songs.

Chapter - 2
The Glory of Pandharpur

A View of Pandharpur

Pandharpur is a prominent pilgrimage town in Mahārāshtra, India, revered for its iconic Vithoba Temple. It is the spiritual hub for millions of devotees of Lord Vithoba, a form of Lord Krishna. This pilgrim town is approximately 210 kms from the city of Pune.

The town is nestled on the banks of the Chandrabhaga River (also known as Bhima) and is considered the "South Kashi" (Southern Varanasi) of Mahārāshtra. Pandharpur was a focal point of the 'Bhakti movement' in medieval India.

Vittal, also known as Vithoba or Panduranga, is a key figure in the Bhakti tradition of Mahārāshtrian saints. He is considered a manifestation of Vishnu or Krishna. The main temple in Pandharpur, dedicated to Vithoba, was probably built in the 12th century by the Yadavas of Devagiri. Some believe that it was built between 1108 and

1152 CE by King Vishnuvardhana of the Hoysala Empire. The temple is known for its beautiful architecture and spiritual ambiance. The architecture of the temple reflects typical Deccan style, with dome motifs and lobed arches though the temple underwent some modifications in later years.

There are many other temples in Pandharpur including one for Rukmini (also called Rakhumayi), the consort of Vittal or Vithoba.

There is a popular legend that traces the origin of Pandharpur temple to a devotee named Pundalik. The story goes that Pundalik, an ardent devotee, was serving his old parents even when Lord Krishna appeared at the door of his home. Pundalik offered a brick for the Lord to stand on while he attended to his parents. Moved by this gesture, Krishna remained in that posture of standing on a brick (*Vit* in Marathi). Thus, the Lord acquired the name of Vittal or Vithoba.

Around Pandharpur

The main shrine of Lord Vittal in Pandharpur is a majestic five-storey structure crowned with a pyramidal spire. At its entrance, statues of Jaya and Vijaya stand in silent guardianship, while inside, Lord Vittal is seen gracefully poised on a brick — an image rich in symbolism. This gesture reflects both Vittal's humility and His eternal devotion to His devotee, Pundalik. The *Vittal ārati* captures this beautifully: *"Yuge aṭṭhāvis, viṭhevari ubhā"* — He has stood on the brick for 28 yugas.

Before entering the temple, devotees traditionally wash their feet in a spring beside the complex as a symbolic act of purification that prepares them for darshan.

Nearby, the Rukmini Mandir stands on a raised platform, dedicated to Rukmini, the consort of Krishna. Uniquely, she is worshipped here separately, believed to be performing penance. The temple, enclosed by high walls and ornate gateways, is entered through the Namdev Gate, named after the saint-poet Sant Namdev, whose image holding a *tambura* adorns the entrance.

Along the banks of the river lies the Vishnupad Mandir, home to a sacred stone slab bearing the lotus footprints of the Lord. These footprints, with one foot gently crossed behind the other, reflect Krishna's divine posture and are revered for their deep spiritual significance.

Pandharpur welcomes pilgrims throughout the year, but the town truly comes alive during the Ekadashi festivals, especially *Ashadhi* (July) and *Kartik Ekadashi (*November), when devotees arrive in vibrant processions. For those seeking a quieter, meditative experience, the cool months from December to February offer a serene and contemplative atmosphere.

Daily Rituals

The Vithoba temple in Pandharpur follows a deeply devoted daily schedule of rituals that include Kakad Aarti, Mahanaivedya, Poshakh, Dhoop Aarti, and Shej Aarti. These rituals are performed at specific times throughout the day, starting before sunrise and concluding after midnight.

Vithoba Temple

The day begins before sunrise with Kakad Aarti, a melodious prayer that symbolizes awakening Lord Vittal, filling the temple premises with divine energy. Devotees gather for Abhishekam (holy bath), where sacred water and offerings purify the idol, symbolizing devotion and surrender. A special offering of food (Mahanaivedyam) to the deity takes place around 11:00 AM. Throughout the day, the deity is worshipped through poojas, bhajans, and darshans by devotees. Late afternoon, alankaram (decoration) is done to the deity with new clothes and ornaments. The evening Dhoop Aarti lights up the sanctum, symbolizing the triumph of light over darkness. The final ritual, Shejarati, is performed before closing, marking the deity's rest for the night.

Pandharpur is a hub of devotion almost throughout the year, with special festivals during Ashadhi Ekadashi (June-July) and Kartiki Ek.

Devotees are generally allowed to touch the feet of the Vithoba idol at the temple in Pandharpur. This uncommon practice is a unique way for devotees to express their reverence and seek blessings from the deity.

Pandharpur hosts the famous **Ashadhi Ekadashi** yatra, drawing millions of devotees (Varkaris) who walk for days from various parts of the state (called "Dindi Yatra"). There is a detailed description of the Varkari tradition elsewhere in this book.

Pandharpur isn't just a pilgrim center - it's an emotion for millions representing devotion without barriers, spiritual unity and simplicity and a living heritage of poetry, and music.

Chapter - 3
Prominent Mahāns of Mahārāshtra

Mahārāshtra has produced many prominent saints who played significant roles in shaping the region's religious and cultural identity. So, it is known as the land of saints.

There are many places for pilgrimage in this land. Travelling through some of these pilgrimage sites offers a unique experience. It provides insight into the immense faith people have in the Supreme, unseen power. The emotions expressed at these sacred centers are not merely a reflection of spirituality but also of profound, implicit devotion.

Among the most revered Mahāns of Mahārāshtra, some of them are prominent. We share a short description of the prominent sants.

1. Sant Dnyaneshwar (1275–1296)

A Display featuring Mahāns of Mahārāshtra

A central figure in the Bhakti movement, Sant Dnyaneshwar is best known for his commentary on the Bhagavad Gita, the "Dnyaneshwari". He also contributed to spiritual and philosophical thought, emphasizing devotion and a personal connection with God.

2. Sant Namdev (1270–1350)

A contemporary of Sant Dnyaneshwar, Namdev was a Varkari saint-poet. *Varkari* is a devotional movement in Mahārāshtra, India, that centers around the worship of Lord Vithoba) whose bhajans and Abhangs (devotional songs) were widely influential. Namdev's teachings emphasized devotion to Lord Vithoba (an incarnation of Vishnu) and the importance of inner purity.

3. Sant Eknath (1533–1599)

Sant Eknath is known for his devotion to Lord Vithoba and for promoting unity among different castes and creeds. His works include translations of the Bhagavad Purana into Marathi and several Abhangs. He emphasized humility, moral discipline, and social equality.

4. Sant Tukaram (1608–1649)

One of the most prominent figures of the Bhakti movement, Sant Tukaram is celebrated for his 'Abhangs' (bhajan songs), which conveyed deep spiritual wisdom through simple language. His unwavering devotion to Lord Vithoba and his messages of compassion, equality, and detachment from materialism resonate to this day.

5. Sant Ramdas (1608–1681)

Also known as Samarth Ramdas, he was a devotee of Lord Rama and Hanuman. He was a spiritual leader as well as a political thinker who inspired Maratha ruler Chhatrapati Shivaji Maharaj. His works, including 'Dasbodh', focus on spiritual guidance, moral behavior, and duty to society.

6. Sant Chokhamela (14th century)

A saint from the Dalit community, Chokhamela was one of the first voices in Indian spirituality to speak against caste discrimination. His devotion to Lord Vithoba, expressed through heartfelt Abhangs, continues to inspire those who fight for social equality.

Later chapters contain more description about these Mahāns. They not only contributed to the spiritual awakening of Mahārāshtra but also played significant roles in social reform, promoting equality, compassion, and devotion. Their legacies continue to inspire millions around the world.

Chapter - 4
The Bhakti Movement

The Sanskrit word *bhakti* derives from the root *bhaj*, meaning "to share, divide, partake, participate, or belong to." Bhakti refers to devotion, love, or attachment to a deity, an enlightened being, or a formless reality. Bhakti is an essential aspect of Hindu spirituality, deeply rooted in a rich tradition of devotion and reverence towards a divine presence. It is a central concept in Indian religions and a key aspect of the Bhakti movement in Hinduism.

Bhakti encompasses various forms, but the common theme is an intense yearning to unite with the object of devotion. This devotion can take different shapes encompassing various forms. Prahlada Maharaja told his father, Hiranyakashipu, about the nine forms of Vishnu-bhakti in the Shrimad Bhagavat Mahapurana (VII.5:23-24). These nine forms of Bhakti include: *Sravana* (listening to the Glory of God), *Kirtana* (singing of His glories), *Smarana* (remembrance of His Name and presence), *Padasevana* (service of His feet), *Archana* (worship of God), *Vandana* (prostration to the Lord), *Dasya* (cultivating the Bhava of a servant with God), *Sakhya* (cultivation of a friendly gesture or Bhava) and *Atmanivedana* (complete surrender of the self).

In Hinduism, Bhakti in any or all forms is viewed as one of the three primary paths to salvation, alongside *Karma* and *Jnana*. *Karma* refers to action or religious duty, where one discharges social and ritual obligations with detachment. *Jnana* signifies knowledge, often through meditation and long-term study, leading to an understanding of the illusory nature of the material world and the non-dual reality of God. *Bhakti*, however, is the path of devotion, emphasizing love for a personal god and self-surrender. It involves the joyous, ecstatic experience of being immersed in the divine presence, transcending intellectual pursuits.

The essence of Bhakti is the pure, eternal love a devotee feels for the object of their devotion, marking it as a deeply spiritual and transformative relationship.

Bhakti cleanses the mind of all its impurities, and consequently, removes the sense of separation or individuality between the seeker and the world. So much importance is given to Bhakti.

Bhakti, as an organized movement in Hinduism, is seen as a response to several social, religious, and philosophical factors during the medieval period in India. It was a reaction to numerous divergent factions that believed in various rituals and casteism. The Bhakti movement emerged as a response to the complexity and exclusion of traditional practices, promoting a simpler option, a personal form of devotion that was inclusive and accessible to all, irrespective of social or caste barriers. It offered a message of spiritual solace, unity, and social equality, calling for devotion to God and compassion for others, irrespective of social status or caste.

There were many great saints in India who were actively involved in the Bhakti movement. They came from different social backgrounds, some very poor, some rich, some scholars, others with little education. Bhakti saints advocated that anyone, regardless of caste or social status, could attain spiritual liberation through sincere devotion. The Bhakti movement emphasized a personal, direct connection with the divine.

The Bhakti movement in India developed gradually, beginning in South India during the 7th to 10th centuries. It was promoted by the Vaishnavite Alvars and Shaivite Nayanars, who traveled and composed hymns dedicated to their gods. Later, in North India, the Bhakti movement found expression through several poets and saints like Kabirdas, Tulsidas, and Mirabai. In East India, a prominent figure was the 12th century poet Jayadeva from Odisha, best known for his *Gita Govinda*, an epic poem that expresses the divine love between Radha and Krishna. In Central India, Mira Bai from Rajasthan was another saint who was born as a princess in a royal Rajput family in 1498, yet her heart and soul belonged to a different realm — one of pure devotion. Though she was married to the prince of Mewar, her love for Krishna eclipsed her royal duties. She became one of the most revered figures in the Bhakti movement, following a rich tradition of devotional poets in medieval India who expressed their boundless love for the divine through human relationships.

Her mystical songs, filled with profound love and yearning, captured the hearts of countless devotees and continue to resonate across northern India to this day. Through her poetic compositions, she transcended the constraints of society, finding her deepest connection with God. Mira Bai's legacy as a Hindu mystic is celebrated not just for her devotion to Krishna, but for her courage to live her truth and express that love with unwavering sincerity.

By the 11th to 15th centuries, the Bhakti movement had grown, fostering a surge in devotional literature both in Sanskrit and regional languages, particularly in the form of hymns, poems, and music. The Bhakti movement also led to far reaching social changes, many of which were brought in by the initiatives of saints from Mahārāshtra.

The Bhakti Movement in Mahārāshtra was centered on the temple of Vithoba or Vittal, the dwelling god of Pandharpur, and regarded as Vishnu's manifestation. Starting sometime in the latter half of the 13th century, the movement progressed rapidly with the active participation of saints. The Echoes of Devotion from the Mahārāshtrian saints reached different parts of India (and now even the globe) spreading the Bhakti Movement far and wide.

The importance of Bhakti is emphasized by Lord Krishna in Bhagavad Gita. He places Bhakti on the top pedestal in the concluding chapter (verse 18.55).

भक्त्या मामभिजानाति यावान्यश्चास्मि तत्त्वतः |
ततो मां तत्त्वतो ज्ञात्वा विशते तदनन्तरम् || 18.55||

bhaktyā mām abhijānāti yāvān yaśh chāsmi tattvataḥ

tato māṁ tattvato jñātvā viśhate tad-anantaram

Meaning: Only by Bhakti -loving devotion to Me does one come to know who I am in Truth. Then, having come to know Me, my devotee enters full consciousness of Me. (The devotee attains me).

Thus, according to Krishna Bhagavan, Bhakti leads one to attain Mukthi (Salvation)!

Chapter - 5
The Role of Mahārāshtrian Mahāns

Background

Hinduism is complex to understand, as it has a diverse range of beliefs, practices, and scriptures. It is also ancient, vast and lacks a single founder. Unlike some religions with a single holy book, Hinduism has a vast collection of scriptures like the Vedas, Upanishads, Puranas, and epics like the Ramayana and Mahabharata. Rituals and practices vary widely across different regions, castes, and communities within Hinduism. It has profound philosophical concepts that can be challenging to grasp for a common man. The worship of numerous deities, each with their own significance and stories, can be overwhelming for anyone.

In Hinduism, attaining 'Brahman' is generally considered the goal of human life. It signifies the realization of one's true self and union with the ultimate reality, often referred to as liberation or moksha. This involves transcending the cycle of birth and death (samsara) and achieving a state of eternal bliss and freedom.

What is Brahman? Brahman is considered as the ultimate, absolute reality, the unchanging, infinite, and all-pervading principle that is the source of all existence. It is often described as the universal essence, and the ultimate truth that underlies all phenomena. While sometimes referred to as God, Brahman transcends the concept of a personal god and is considered the fundamental reality of the universe.

Brahman, the ultimate reality, is understood in two primary ways: *Saguna Brahman,* which is Brahman with attributes (form, qualities), and *Nirguna Brahman*, which is Brahman without attributes (formless, beyond qualities). Saguna Brahman is often associated with deities like

Vishnu, Shiva, or Devi, while Nirguna Brahman is the absolute, formless, and indescribable reality.

In Hindu philosophy, *Jnana Yoga* (path of knowledge) and *Bhakti Yoga* (path of devotion) are two distinct paths leading to spiritual liberation. Jnana Yoga emphasizes self-realization through knowledge and understanding, while Bhakti Yoga focuses on loving devotion to a personal God. While seemingly different, both paths aim for the same goal – attainment of the divine.

Spiritual Landscape

With such complexities, it is difficult for a common man to understand Hindu religion. In 12th/13th centuries, the spiritual landscape of India, particularly in Mahārāshtra, was characterized by a rigid social structure and limited access to spiritual knowledge.

Spiritual and philosophical knowledge was primarily confined to the elite, who studied Sanskrit texts like the Vedas and Upanishads, while women and lower castes were excluded.

The Role of Māhāns

Beginning with Sant Dnyaneshwar in the 13th century, a series of Māhāns in Mahārāshtra played a pivotal role in transforming the spiritual landscape and democratizing spirituality by making their teachings accessible to all in the local language of Marathi.

The Māhāns of Mahārāshtra brought forth a philosophy of integrating the two paths of jnAna (knowledge) and bhakti (devotion). In simple words, they brought a realization that the ultimate Brahman, both Saguna and Nirguna – with attributes and without attributes, are one and the same. The Māhāns of Mahārāshtra proved that through sheer bhakti of Love, anyone can reach the Saguna Brahman. To reach the Nirguna Brahman (Formless) is a lot more difficult due to lack of visualizing a form. For the former, there is any one of the nine methods known as *Navadha Bhakti*, which are classical forms to express devotion to a deity.

The Mahārāshtra Bhakti saints practised the nine forms of bhakti, although they emphasized personal devotion and love for the deity above all else. While they acknowledged and sometimes incorporated elements of the nine forms, their focus was on a more direct and personal relationship with God, often through simple acts of devotion and love.

To reach the Impersonal Ultimate one needs to discipline oneself through the three-fold ascent of Śravaṇa (listening), Manana (deliberation on what has been learnt) and Nididhyāsana (the analysis and synthesis of the accrued knowledge). These Māhāns shared some common characteristics:

1. **Spiritual Inclusivity:** Māhāns like Dnyaneshwar, Tukaram, and Namdev emphasized devotion to God regardless of caste or social status. Their teachings promoted a more inclusive approach to spirituality, encouraging people from various backgrounds to participate in religious practices. They contributed significantly to the "Bhakti movement" across India, which became a pan-Indian spiritual revolution. This movement emphasized personal, direct devotion (bhakti) to the Almighty without intermediaries like priests or rituals. The concept of 'Bhakti' helped to transcend rigid caste divisions and made spiritual practices accessible to ordinary people, regardless of caste, gender, or education.

2. **Social Reform:** Many saints challenged the rigid caste system and social injustices that existed in their time. For instance, Tukaram's verses often criticized societal norms that marginalized the lower castes, fostering a sense of equality and urging social reform. Sant Chokhamela, a saint from a so-called "untouchable" caste, became a revered figure, showing that spiritual greatness was not confined to caste hierarchy.

3. **Literary Contributions:** The saints produced a rich body of literature in Marathi, making spiritual and philosophical ideas accessible to the common people. By composing religious texts and poetry in Marathi, Maharashtrian saints empowered the local people to approach the divine directly through personal devotion, prayers, and singing, fostering a more inclusive spiritual atmosphere. This also helped to elevate the Marathi language and culture, fostering a sense of regional identity.

4. **Community and Devotion:** The Māhāns established a culture of collective worship and community gatherings, which brought people together, strengthened social bonds, and promoted a sense of belonging among diverse groups. The Varkari tradition, for instance, emphasizes pilgrimage, communal singing, and collective worship, which became integrated into broader Hindu practices. The worship of Vithoba (Vittal) worship centered on the temple in Pandharpur — became a major devotional focus, influencing Hindu pilgrimage practices and creating a strong devotional culture that is still vibrant today.

5. **Moral and Ethical Values:** The teachings of these saints emphasized virtues like humility, compassion, and selflessness. This contributed to shaping the moral framework of society and encouraged individuals to lead more ethical lives. The Mahāns of Mahārāshtra promoted non-materialistic and ethical living, reinforced the importance of moral behavior alongside religious observance. Their influence also highlighted the idea that true spirituality lay not in outward rituals but in inner transformation and self-realization, which became a key concept in Hindu philosophy.

6. **Resistance to Oppression:** The Māhāns often stood against oppressive regimes and practices, inspiring movements for social justice and equality. Their teachings encouraged people to question authority and advocate for their rights.

Overall, the Māhāns of Mahārāshtra played a crucial role in shaping a more egalitarian and spiritually rich society, leaving a legacy that continues to influence Mahārāshtra's cultural and social landscape today. Their teachings continue to inspire Hindus across the world, emphasizing inclusivity, social justice, and devotion over ritualism, which has contributed to a more personal and egalitarian approach to spirituality in Hinduism.

Chapter - 6
Sant Dnyaneshwar

Sant Dnyaneshwar, also known as Jnaneshwar, Jnanadeva, Dnyandev, Mauli, or Dnyaneshwar Vittal Kulkarni, was born in the year 1275. He was an Indian Marathi saint, poet, thinker, and yogi who belonged to the Varkari and Nath Shaiva traditions. In a short span 21 years, he made profound contributions to the Bhakti movement and Marathi literature. He is one of the pioneers of the Varkari (Vithoba – Krishna) Bhakti cult tradition of Hinduism in Mahārāshtra, and his legacy influenced saint-poets like Eknath and Tukaram.

The name "Dnyaneshwar," pronounced as *gyaa·nay·shvuhr*, is derived from two Sanskrit words: "Dnyan," meaning knowledge or wisdom, and "Ishwar," meaning Lord or God. Thus, Dnyaneshwar can be interpreted as "Lord of Knowledge" or "God of Wisdom," and he is affectionately referred to as Jnaneshwar Maharaj.

Dnyaneshwar was born on the auspicious day of Krishna Janmashtami in the year 1275 CE in a Marathi-speaking Deshastha Brahman family in Apegaon hamlet on the banks of the Godavari River close to Paithan in Mahārāshtra.

Dnyaneshwar's father Vittalpant was a Kulkarni, a Brahmin hereditary accountant, who kept land and tax records in villages in Apegaon. He had inherited this occupation from his forefathers. His wife Rakhumabai was the daughter of the Kulkarni of Alandi, near Pune. Vittalpant was a very pious man. He had lost his parents at a young age. He had no children. Becoming disenchanted with life, he decided to abandon his materialistic life. He moved to Kashi (now Varanasi) and found a spiritual instructor.

Without consulting his wife, he made the decision there to become a Sanyasi (monk). His spiritual guide Rama Sharma, also known as Ramananda, initiated him into Sanyasa Ashram. When the Guru Rama Sharma came to know that Vittalpant was already married and had abandoned his family to become a monk, he ordered him to return to his wife and carry out his responsibilities as a householder.

Following the guru's command, Vittalpant returned home and started living with his wife in Alandi. In due course, Rakhumabai gave birth to four children: Nivruttinath (1273 CE), Dnyaneshwar (1275 CE), Sopan (1277 CE), and Muktabai (1279 CE).

A Sanyasi (monk) reverting to his life as a householder was not acceptable to the traditional local Brahmins. Vittalpant faced a great deal of ridicule and pressure from the Brahmin community. The community refused to treat Vittalpant and his family as part of Brahmin sect and did not permit Dnyaneshwar and his brothers to participate in the Upanayanam (holy thread) rituals. Facing social and spiritual ostracization from the local Brahmins, Vittalpant moved with his family to Nashik.

Dnyaneshwar was deeply affected by the injustices faced by his family and took up the spiritual path early in his life, despite his young age. His father's life and death played a crucial role in shaping the spiritual journey of Dnyaneshwar. He became the first known philosopher to write in the Marathi language.

Dnyaneshwari or Bhavarta Deepika

Most local people in those days did not understand the teachings of the Bhagavad Gita as it was in Sanskrit language. However, Sant Dnyaneshwar wanted the people to appreciate the wisdom the Gita. So, he started explaining the Gita in simple Marathi that appealed to the local people. It was the first time that people heard someone tell them the contents of the Gita in their understandable language of Marathi. Soon, crowds gathered to listen to Sant Dnyaneshwar. To reach the masses, Sant Dnyaneshwar translated the Bhagavad Gita into Marathi into a book form and named it 'Bhavarta Deepika' (Light on the Inner Meaning). The most surprising thing is that Dnyaneshwar was about fourteen years old when he did this remarkable work. This book became a foundational text for the Varkari sect and is highly regarded for making the teachings of the Gita accessible to the common people. It is celebrated widely for its poetic beauty and philosophical depth.

Other Saints

During Dnyaneshwar's time, there were many other saints too. There was Narhari Sonar, a goldsmith; Gora Kumbhar, a potter; Janabai, a servant maid; - all common people pursuing different professions to make a living. They all joined together and formed a pilgrim's group which came to be called 'Varkari.' They were exceptional devotees who had implicit faith in Pandurang Vittal. Their devotional songs echoed throughout Mahārāshtra. The leader of this Varkari group was Sant Dnyaneshwar. Later, we will describe more about the Varkari Tradition that continues to this day.

Mass Appeal

The saints were simple selfless people who were united in their devotion to Vittal. They appealed to the masses who respected them and called them 'Sants.' People extended a warm welcome to them wherever they went. Such a humble and united group was rare and not seen elsewhere in those days. Not only they spread devotion but also contributed to Marathi literature.

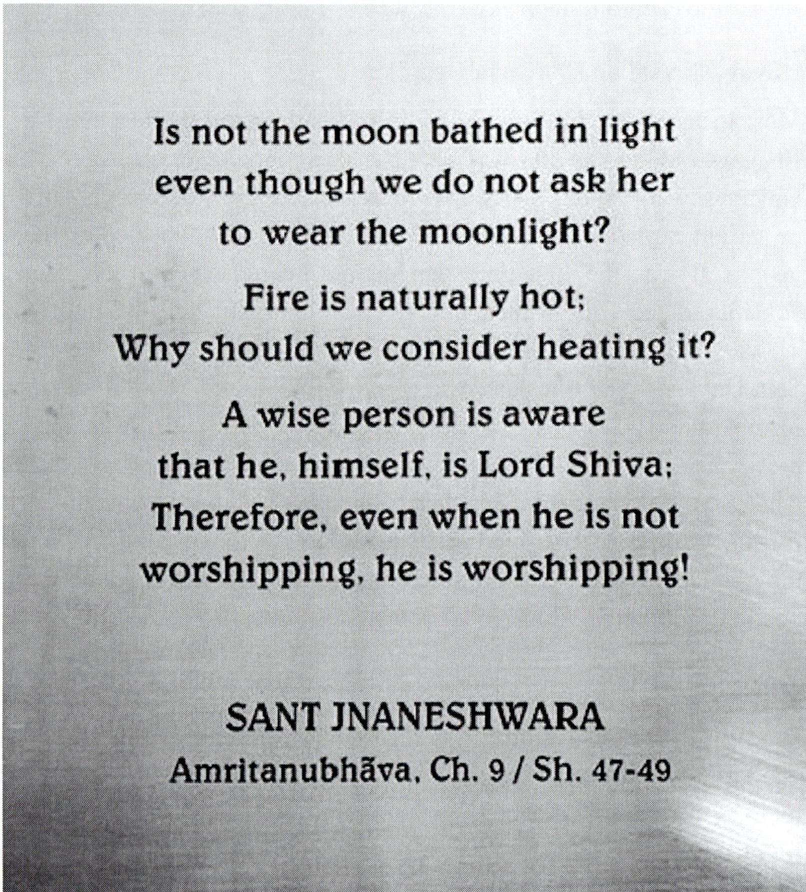
Is not the moon bathed in light
even though we do not ask her
to wear the moonlight?

Fire is naturally hot;
Why should we consider heating it?

A wise person is aware
that he, himself, is Lord Shiva;
Therefore, even when he is not
worshipping, he is worshipping!

SANT JNANESHWARA
Amritanubhāva, Ch. 9 / Sh. 47-49

In addition to the "Dnyaneshwari," Dnyaneshwar authored various devotional poems that conveyed his spiritual insights and devotion to God, leaving a lasting impact on Marathi literature and devotional practices. His teachings emphasized devotion, simplicity, and a deep understanding of the divine, advocating that true spiritual knowledge transcends ritualistic practices and is attained through devotion and inner realization

Bhakti Movement

Dnyaneshwar was a pivotal figure in the Bhakti movement, which emphasized personal devotion to God and the equality of all individuals, regardless of caste or social status. His teachings inspired many followers and played a crucial role in the spread of the Bhakti tradition throughout Mahārāshtra and beyond.

The enduring influence of his teachings continues to inspire spiritual seekers today. The "Dnyaneshwari" remains widely read and revered, and Dnyaneshwar is celebrated as a leading figure in India's devotional and philosophical traditions.

Sant Dnyaneshwar's contributions have left a lasting impact on both religious thought and literary culture in India, solidifying his status as a central figure in the history of the Bhakti movement.

Dnyaneshwar had several siblings, including his elder brother, Nivrutti Nath, and his younger siblings, Sopan and Muktabai. They were all notable figures in the Bhakti movement and contributed to Marathi literature and spirituality.

Miracles

Sant Dnyaneshwar is revered not only for his spiritual insights and literary contributions but also for the miracles attributed to him. While the primary focus of his life and teachings is on his philosophical and devotional work, there are several accounts of miracles associated with him that are cherished in the tradition. Some notable miracles attributed to Sant Dnyaneshwar include the following:

1. The miracle of Sant Dnyaneshwar making a buffalo recite the Vedas is a well-known story that illustrates his spiritual prowess and deep understanding of the sacred texts.

   According to a legendary story, when Dnyaneshwar was a young boy, he encountered a group of hostile brahmins who refused to accept him in their community as his father had returned to Gṛhasthaashram (family life) after becoming a Sanyasin (one who has renounced the family).

Dnyaneshwar said, "When nothing exists outside the One infinite Brahman, my Atman is no different from yours or from that passing buffalo!"

On hearing this, the pundits were greatly amused and taunted the boy saying, "If the buffalo is as much a part of the Atman as you, let us hear him recite the Vedas."

"So be it," said Dnyaneshwar. He took up the challenge, turned to the buffalo, asked him gently: "If the True Self which resides in all things abides in you, speak the truth to all present." Then, he began to recite a passage of the Rig Veda, extolling the inner meaning of the word "AUM," when the buffalo took over and completed the verses in a deep and clear voice.

"Forgive us," cried the Head Pundit, "We have been steeped in ignorance and arrogance. You are truly a saint and an Avatar of Divine Knowledge! We humbly beseech you to forgive us." The pundits gave him the place of honor and carried him in a procession.

2. Some stories recount that Dnyaneshwar performed miraculous healings. It is believed that he had the power to cure ailments and provide relief to those who were suffering, often through his blessings and prayers.

3. There is another story about Dnyaneshwar taming an egoistic yogi named Chang Deva. The yogi had many mystical powers which took the people by awe. Once, riding a fierce tiger, with a cobra for a whip and his long-matted locks beating the air, he approached the little valley cradling Alandi, like a raging tornado. People gathered in a crowd to see him.

   At that time, Dnyaneshwar, Nivrutti, Sopan and Mukta were seated on a wall, enjoying the evening breeze. "What is this commotion up there in the hills?" asked Mukta. "This is Chang Deva yogi coming forward riding his huge tiger," said Dnyaneshwar. So, all three said: "Why don't we go and welcome him?" "Right," answered Dnyaneshwar. "We ought to go and greet the ancient one and show him our respect." Saying this, Dnyaneshwar patted the wall with his hand and ordered it gently, "Come on, O wall, rise and carry us towards the yogi." When Chang Deva saw four figures riding a brick wall, he hurriedly got down from his tiger and threw himself at Dnyaneshwar's feet and pleaded forgiveness for his pride and ignorance.

Muktabai became Chang Deva's guru, imparting lessons on true renunciation and the ability to rise above the distinctions of name and form. Her poetry is considered one of the treasures of Marathi literature.

4. Samadhi in Alandi: One of the most profound miracles attributed to Dnyaneshwar is his samadhi (final resting place) in Alandi. His samadhi shrine (see picture) in Alandi is considered a sacred site, and many devotees believe that the site itself has miraculous qualities, reflecting Dnyaneshwar's divine presence.

The miracles serve multiple purposes: It highlights Dnyaneshwar's extraordinary abilities, emphasizes the idea that spiritual wisdom is not confined to humans, and critiques the rigid caste and class structures of society. The story symbolizes the belief that true knowledge and divinity can manifest unexpected forms, reinforcing the inclusive nature of the Bhakti movement.

In those days, India was made up of numerous small states mostly ruled by kings. The local kingdom with Devagiri as its capital was relatively peaceful and stable, and the king was a supporter of the arts and literature.

During Dnyaneshwar's time, the benevolent King Ramadevarao ruled, a great patron of learning who generously endowed the magnificent temple of Panduranga in Pandharpur with wealth. He is mentioned by Dnyaneshwar towards the end of his seminal work, the "Dnyaneshwari".

His Teachings

Sant Dnyaneshwar employed rich imagery to convey the profound truths of Vedanta, making the concepts of Purusha and Prakriti accessible to ordinary people. He emphasized the importance of understanding one's purpose in life and ultimate goals. Dnyaneshwar greatly valued humility, providing a deep analysis of the humble man who may be a self-realized soul, withdrawn from worldly concerns. He describes such a person as living in solitude, befriending the wind, conversing with the sky, and cherishing the trees as dearly as himself. A humble individual recognizes all beings, from the tiniest ant to the highest God, as part of the same self. Dnyaneshwar expresses his profound sense of oneness and peace, highlighting the harmony of one who is liberated from selfishness and in tune with nature.

“The realized man is never affected by sorrow or suffering,” Dnyaneshwar states. “Like the vast ocean, he can accommodate rivers of grief without being disturbed. He is so friendly with the world that he cannot distinguish between himself and others.”

Sant Dnyaneshwar held the Guru in the highest regard, stating, “Without unwavering faith in the Guru, one achieves nothing. The Guru resides in one's heart like a fixed star, where he is worshiped incessantly.”

The core of his teachings may be summarized as, *“The essence of true knowledge is self-realization. When the mind, the soul, and the body are in harmony, one attains peace.”*

Sant Namdev was a contemporary of Sant Dnyaneshwar, and the two shared a close bond, enjoying each other’s company. Both embarked on a pilgrimage to the North, accompanied by several other saints, spreading their teachings along the way.

Upon their return to Pandharpur, Sant Dnyaneshwar unexpectedly declared his intention to leave the world through a voluntary act of deep samadhi at Alandi.

Despite his friends and followers' attempts to dissuade him, he maintained that his mission was complete, and it was time for him to depart.

Sanjeevan Samadhi

Sanjeevan Samadhi in Alandi

Namdev recounts the events in detail. A pit was dug to the left of the Siddheshwar temple, beneath an Ajana tree. A mat of Kusa grass was spread and covered with deer skin. The crowd sang kirtans for three continuous days and nights.

Afterward, Dnyaneshwar bathed in the Indrayani River. Clad in saffron cloth, he descended the steps into the pit, saluted the ten directions, and prayed silently. Sitting cross-legged with his hands on his knees, he entered deep meditation, drawing up his life force in stages while discarding his physical body. As he reached the final state of samadhi, Dnyaneshwar blissfully merged with the Infinite.

Thus, at the young age of 21, on the thirteenth day of the dark fortnight of Kartika in the year 1296, Sant Dnyaneshwar attained 'Sanjeevan Samadhi' in Alandi on the banks of the Indrayani River. Sanjeevan Samadhi is a kind of yoga where an individual voluntarily enters a state of deep meditation that ultimately leads to the cessation of the physical body. His Samadhi is in the Siddhesvara Temple complex in Alandi.

Sant Dnyaneshwar had fully conquered himself and guided countless souls on the path to God-realization. Even to this day, he is celebrated for his profound contributions to Marathi literature and the Bhakti movement. His samadhi shrine in Alandi has become a major pilgrimage site for his devotees.

Chapter - 7
Sant Eknath

Sant Eknath was born around the year 1533 in Paithan, a town in Mahārāshtra, in the Rigvedi Brahmin family of a great saint known as Sant Bhanudas. Eknath's parents were Suryanaryana and Rukmanibai. He lost his parents while he was a child and was raised by his grandparents. He was probably named 'Eknath' as he was the only descendent in the family.

From an early age, Eknath exhibited deep religious devotion and an inclination toward spirituality. He realized that he could not progress spiritually unless he had a Guru. The story goes that he heard a divine voice in a nearby Shiva temple directing him to meet a person named Janardana Pant in Devgad. So, one day he left for Devgad and met with Janardana Swami who was a devotee of Dattatreya. Following this meeting, Eknath became a disciple of Janardana Swami, a respected saint and scholar, who taught him Vedanta, Yoga, and Bhakti. With Janardana Swami's guidance, Eknath studied both many Sanskrit scriptures and learnt the philosophy of devotion. Later, Eknath went on a spiritual pilgrimage to Kashi (now Varanasi), where he sharpened his understanding of the Vedas and Upanishads.

Following the Varkari tradition, Eknath's devotion was directed toward Vithoba of Pandharpur. He composed many devotional songs, in praise of Vittal. Over 300 Abhangs are popularly attributed to him. These are lyrical, spiritual poems in praise of Lord Vittal (Pandurang), often sung during pilgrimages and bhajans. His style is marked by simple words reflecting emotional depth and conveying a universal message of devotion.

One of his well-known Abhangs beginning with 'Kāyā hī Paṇḍharī' drips with devotion. We share the lyrics of it here in both Marathi and English with the meaning.

काया ही पंढरी आत्मा हा विठ्ठल ।

नांदतो केवळ पांडुरंग ॥१॥

Kāyā hī Paṇḍharī, ātmā hā Viṭṭhala |

Nāndato kevaḷa Pāṇḍuraṅga ||1||

My body is Pandhari and my soul is Vittal. Only Panduranga dwells inside me.

भाव-भक्ति भीमा उदक ते वाहे ।

बरवा शोभताहे पांडुरंग ॥२॥

Bhāva-bhakti Bhīmā udaka te vāhe |

Baravā śobhatāhe Pāṇḍuraṅga ||2||

My faith and devotion in Panduranga is like flowing water of Bheema river.

दया क्षमा शांती हेंचि वाळुवंट ।

मिळालासे थाट वैष्णवांचा ॥३॥

Dayā-kṣamā-śānti hechi vāḷuvaṇṭa |

Miḷālāse thāṭa vaiṣṇavāñchā ||3||

Compassion, Forgiveness and Peace in our heart is like gathering of Vaishnavites on the sands of Chandra Bhaga River.

ज्ञान ध्यान पूजा विवेक आनंद ।

हाचि वेणुनाद शोभतसे ॥४॥

Jñāna-dhyāna-pūjā viveka ānanda |

Hāci veṇunāda śobhatase ||4||

Awareness, Meditation, Prayer and Prudence are my happiness like notes emanating from Krishna's flute.

दश इंद्रियांचा एक मेळ केला ।

ऐसा गोपाळकाला होत असे ॥५॥

Daśa indriyāñchā eka meḷa kelā |

Aisā Gopāḷakālā hot ase ||5||

I have gathered all ten of my organs of senses (five Jnanendriyas) and of actions (Karmendriyas) that is my offering to the Lord.

देखिली पंढरी देहीं-जनी-वनीं ।

एका जनार्दनी वारी करी ॥६॥

Dekhīlī Paṇḍharī dehīṃ-janīṃ-vanīṃ |

Ekā Janārdanī vāri karī ||6||

Eknath says, I see the sanctity of Pandhari in Myself, in People and in all surroundings. That is the place of pilgrimage inside us.

It is clear from Verse 6 that Eknath identifies himself with the Paramatma- the Super soul of Pandari. It is the core of Advaitha Philosophy. This divine Abhang is melodiously sung by the famous singer Pandit Bhimsen Joshi.

Eknath's teachings emphasized pure devotion (bhakti) over ritualism, believing that love and surrender to God were more important than performing elaborate religious rituals.

One of his most significant works is the 'Eknathi Bhagavata,' a Marathi commentary on the 11th Skanda (cantos) of 'Srimad Bhagavatam'-a most ancient scripture in Sanskrit. He wrote it in simple Marathi, making the spiritual teachings accessible and easily understandable to common people. Eknath also translated and commented on the famous epic 'Ramayana' in Marathi and named it as 'Bhavarth Ramayana.'

This work covered the moral and spiritual lessons of Lord Rama's life, again making complex religious teachings accessible to a wider audience. Through this work, Eknath promoted Bhakti, ethical living, and devotion to God as the primary paths to salvation.

Like most other saints of the Bhakti movement, Eknath was a philosopher and a social reformer. His philosophy was rooted in the belief that God resides in every living being, and he advocated for the equality of all humans.

He firmly opposed the caste system and untouchability that were prevalent in society. Eknath worked to bridge the gap between different communities and bring people together in their devotion to God. His emphasis on love, compassion, and service to others resonated well with the common people. He is regarded as one of the key saints in the Varkari tradition that centers around the worship of Vittal, the deity of Pandharpur. Eknath made significant contributions to the Marathi language too through his religious literature.

On his personal side, Eknath was known for his patience, humility, and compassion. Stories of his life often highlight his kindness toward the downtrodden and his ability to see divinity in all beings.

Sant Eknath's teachings and works continue to be an integral part of Mahārāshtra's spiritual and cultural heritage. His compositions, particularly his Abhangs, are still remembered and sung by Varkaris during the annual pilgrimage to Pandharpur and at other devotional gatherings.

Chapter - 8
Sant Namdev

Sant Namdev, also called Namdeva or Namdeo, was a prominent 13th-14th century saint and poet from Mahārāshtra, India. Namdev was born on a Sunday, in the Shukla Ekadeshi of Kartika of the year 1270, five years before Dnyaneshwar, in the village of Narasapur, which is now part of the Pune district in Mahārāshtra. He was born to a couple named Damasheti and Gonabhai, who were devoted Vaishnavas. His early life was marked by deep devotion to Lord Vithoba.

He came from a humble family, and his early life was marked by deep devotion and a simple lifestyle. He is revered as a key figure in the Bhakti movement, which emphasized devotion to God over ritualistic practices.

Eknath offering food to Vittal

When Namadeva was five years old, his mother sent him to the temple with some food to offer to God as Naivedyam. Nama Deva placed the dish before the deity, Shri Vittal, and asked Him to eat it. Confused and upset when the stone deity did not respond, Nama Deva pleaded with Vittal to take the food. (See inset picture). In his frustration, he threatened to break his head on the floor if the food wasn't consumed. At that moment, Vittal appeared, smiling and took the food. Nama Deva returned home and told his mother that Vittal had eaten the food, but she did not believe him and thought he was lying.

The next day, Nama Deva's father, Damasheti, followed his son to the temple to witness what happened. Again, Vittal ate the food, and Damasheti saw the divine act. He fell at Vittal's feet, and the deity blessed both father and son, instructing them not to share what they had witnessed.

Namadev was married at a young age to Rajaibai. His wife too visited the temple with him and prayed to Vittal not to take her husband away from her. Namdev dedicated himself completely to God and His service. His songs ever more intense and beautiful were repeated in all corners of the land and whoever came to Pandharpur, first bowed to Namdev, God's own beloved devotee. Vittal directed Namdev to a Guru who was Visoba Khechara, a disciple of young Sant Dnyaneshwar. So, Namdev got an opportunity to meet with Sant Dnyaneshwar. When Sant Dnyaneshwar requested Namdev to accompany him on a trip to the North, he first recoiled at the idea of leaving his beloved Lord Panduranga. Sant Dnyaneshwar insisted. Namdev asked Panduranga who told him to follow Dnyaneshwar and remember Him wherever he went.

Throughout his life, Namdev displayed a profound devotion to Vittal and a deep sense of spirituality. He was influenced by the teachings of the Bhakti movement and dedicated himself to singing and composing devotional hymns.

Some of his major accomplishments and contributions to the community include:

1. Abhangs (Devotional Songs)

Namdev composed thousands of Abhangs, devotional hymns in Marathi sung in praise of Lord Vithoba. These are simple yet deeply spiritual compositions, reflecting intense devotion and love for God.

The Abhangs express Namdev's ideas of equality, devotion, and the futility of rituals in attaining God. His poetry often speaks of a deep yearning for divine connection and the ultimate unity of the soul with the divine.

2. Contribution to Sikhism

Over sixty of Namdev's hymns are included in the *'Guru Granth Sahib'*, the sacred scripture of Sikhism, making him one of the fifteen Bhagats whose hymns are part of the Sikh holy text.

His hymns in the Guru Granth Sahib often focus on devotion, the oneness of God, and the rejection of caste distinctions.

3. Philosophy of Bhakti

Namdev advocated for '*Nirguna Bhakti'* (devotion to a formless God), which goes beyond idol worship, focusing on God as omnipresent and transcendent. However, he maintained a personal devotion to Vithoba, symbolizing the coexistence of both '*Saguna'* (with form) and '*Nirguna*' (without form) aspects of divinity in his teachings.

4. Social Reform and Equality

Namdev's works frequently criticized the caste system and ritualistic practices. He believed in the equality of all individuals regardless of caste, gender, or social status.

His poetry often spoke against the superficial distinctions of caste, emphasizing that God's grace is accessible to everyone.

5. Influence on the Bhakti Movement

As a key figure in the 'Varkari' tradition (a devotional movement dedicated to Vithoba), Namdev's teachings influenced the larger Bhakti movement across India.

His devotion, combined with his progressive social ideals, helped bridge the gap between the high-born and the low-born, bringing people together through the common bond of love for God.

6. Philosophical Dialogues

Namdev's poetry often includes conversations with God or philosophical reflections, offering a direct and intimate perspective on divine-human relationships.

Through his poetic works and devotion, Sant Namdev not only spread the message of love for God but also challenged the social and religious orthodoxy of his time, making his teachings timeless and influential across different traditions. His followers continue to revere him for his spiritual insights and contributions to devotional music and poetry.

Sant Namdev's hymns and teachings continue to inspire people across different regions and religions. His contributions to devotional literature and his emphasis on a personal, loving relationship with God have made him a cherished figure in Indian spiritual history. His life and work are celebrated for their profound impact on devotional practices and his role in promoting the values of love, humility, and inclusiveness in spirituality.

While his primary legacy lies in his spiritual teachings and literary works, there are also stories of miracles attributed to him. These miracles often serve to highlight his deep spiritual connection and divine favor. Many stories recount his ability to heal the sick, provide for the needy, and even demonstrate divine intervention during challenging times. His deep devotion and unwavering faith are often seen as the source of these miraculous events, reflecting his connection with the divine.

One of the most famous miracles associated with Sant Namdev involves his ability to provide food for the needy. According to legend, during a time of famine, he miraculously transformed a small amount of food into enough to feed a large crowd of hungry people. This act demonstrated not only his compassion but also his deep connection with the divine.

Another notable miracle is his encounter with a devotee who was ill. It is said that Namdev prayed for the devotee's health, and they were healed instantly, showcasing his power as a saint and healer.

These stories not only highlight his spiritual prowess but also reflect the themes of devotion and service central to his teachings. Namdev is believed to have lived a life fully dedicated to spiritual practice and service. He passed away around 1350 CE, and his samadhi (final resting place) is in the city of Panjim in Goa, where a shrine dedicated to him is a site of pilgrimage for his devotees.

Chapter - 9
Sant Tukaram

Sant Tukaram, the revered 17th-century Marathi saint and poet, was born to a couple named Bhanji Pundalik and Satyabhama, of Dehu, near Pune, in Mahārāshtra. They were devout followers of Lord Vithoba (also called Pandurang) and played a significant role in shaping Tukaram's spiritual journey. His family background and early life experiences greatly influenced his later teachings and compositions.

Sant Tukaram's parents were Kumbis (potters) by profession. The Kumbis were traditionally involved in pottery and earthenware crafts, which is significant in the context of Tukaram's life and teachings, as he often emphasized humility and devotion over social status.

Tukaram’s early life was full of struggles. A great famine occurred in Mahārāshtra in 1630 CE causing widespread distress. This famine remains one of the most devastating famines in the history of India.

His parents died a few years before the famine. Following the famine, Tukaram faced significant personal hardships, including the loss of his first wife and children, which deepened his spiritual quest. His bullocks too died, his lands were sold to pay his debts and there was nothing left. He lost everything including his reputation, money, business, cattle and land and he became destitute. In despair, he threw into the river Indrayani all his account books and retired to a lonely place in Pandharpur. “Panduranga, nothing stands now between us two!” he sang.

From then on, Tukaram’s devotion to Pandurang increased day by day until the world seemed to exist no more for him. He composed heart-rending poems of longing for God and songs of praise and love for his Lord.

The Entrance to Tukaram Samsthan, Dehu

Tukaram held kirtans (devotional singing programs) in Dehu, and Pune where people gathered in great numbers. They noticed his saintly appearance and started repeating his touching songs while they went about performing their daily chores. Women sang as when they were grinding millets, rice or some others while they were drawing water from the wells, and men sang while ploughing in the fields.

At his birthplace in Dehu, some of Tukaram's hand-written Abhangs are still preserved in a glass case.

All this popularity of Tukaram had caused jealousy to a learned Brahmin called Rameshwar Bhat.

He told people that Tukaram's Abhangs were against the Vedas and other holy scriptures and so, they should be thrown in the river. Tukaram obeyed the pandit's order, wrapped up his writings, tied them to a stone and threw it into the Indrayani River. This act broke his heart, and he fasted on the banks of the river to give up his life. He was continuously singing "Vittal, Vittal, Panduranga," and on the thirteenth day, a miracle happened. The missing parcel of Abhangs surfaced on the water and came up to the shore. A cry of joy rose, and Tukaram was carried home to be feasted and worshipped by the whole town.

However, the pandit was not pleased. He continued to harass Tukaram. It so happened he contracted a skin disease. He went to Alandi and prayed at Sant Dnynaneshwar's samadhi for relief. The Holy Sant appeared in his dream and ordered him to seek surrender at Tukaram's feet. So, at last, giving up his stubborn pride, the Pandit reached Dehu and fell before Tukaram. Tukaram lifted him gently and at the touch of his hands, the misery of Rameshwar Bhat subsided entirely. From then on, Rameshwar Bhat became Tukaram's devoted disciple, and one of those who recorded the events of his life.

This background contributed to his deep connection with the common people and his impactful spiritual message.

Tukaram's Contributions

Sant Tukaram made significant contributions to spirituality, literature, and social reform. Here are some key aspects of his contributions:

1. **Literary Contributions:** Tukaram composed thousands of Abhangs, expressing deep spiritual insights and emotions. His poetry often challenged social norms and promoted the idea of a personal relationship with God. (You can read some of his Abhangs in this book)

2. **Philosophical Influence:** He emphasized the importance of devotion (bhakti) over ritualistic practices, advocating for a direct connection with the divine.

3. **Social Reform:** Tukaram's teachings addressed issues of caste and inequality, promoting a message of unity and equality among all people.

4. **Integration of Music and Dance:** He popularized the use of music in devotional practices, influencing the tradition of 'Kirtan' (devotional singing) in Mahārāshtra. To this day, the practice of public singing of Kirtans continues. Tukaram's music have been translated into English in a book titled 'The Poems of Tukarama' by J. Nelson Fraser and K.B. Marathe published by Motilal Banarsidass Books, Delhi.

Interaction with Chhatrapati Shivaji Maharaj

Tukaram reached the height of his fame as a saint of Mahārāshtra concurrently with Shivaji's attainment in his own sphere as a King and the founder of the Maratha Empire.

Chhatrapati Shivaji Maharaj was deeply influenced by spiritual figures like Sant Tukaram. Tukaram's devotion to Lord Vithoba (Pandurang) and his message of equality, humility, and devotion resonated with Shivaji Maharaj who then was striving to establish a kingdom based on dharma (righteousness). It is said that Shivaji Maharaj had many interesting interactions with Sant Tukaram. Their relationship is seen as one of mutual respect and spiritual admiration. Although the exact details of their meetings aren't well-documented, there are several legends and stories that highlight their connection.

Shivaji Maharaj meets Sant Tukaram

One popular account suggests that Shivaji Maharaj once visited Sant Tukaram to seek his blessings. Despite being a warrior king, Shivaji is said to have humbly approached Tukaram as a disciple, recognizing the saint's spiritual greatness. Sant Tukaram, known for his humility and disinterest in material power, reportedly blessed Shivaji but declined any royal offerings or honors.

Tukaram's spiritual influence helped strengthen Shivaji's resolve in his mission of establishing a just and righteous kingdom. Shivaji, in turn, greatly respected Tukaram and the Bhakti movement, which promoted devotion to God and transcended caste and social boundaries.

Their interaction symbolizes the link between spirituality and governance, where a king seeks wisdom and guidance from a saint, aligning his leadership with spiritual principles.

Sant Tukaram inspires

Tukaram declared, “A saint devotes himself entirely to the happiness of others, his worship consists of helping his fellow beings. He rests his mind on the feet of God and asks for nothing.”

True to his words, he gave plentifully to all who came to him seeking his blessings.

The great Indian scholar Dr. R.D. Ranade said:

“Tukaram exhibits all the doubts and disbeliefs, the weaknesses and the sufferings, the anxieties and the uncertainties, through which every aspiring soul must pass, before he can come into the life of Light, Spirit and Harmony. There is no other instance in the whole galaxy of the Maratha Saints, barring perhaps Namadeva, which can be regarded as illustrative of this human element which we find in Tukaram.”

No wonder, Tukaram's life and teachings continue to inspire millions, and he is regarded as one of the foremost saints in the Bhakti movement, with a lasting impact on Marathi culture and spirituality.

One of the lessons we learn from Tukaram is that we are deeply influenced by the company we keep. Tukaram taught that spiritual companionship or Satsang can nurture our well-being and support our efforts.

Tukaram departing to Vaikuntam

Tukaram's devotion to Vittal was so extraordinary that he attained Mukti by constantly repeating Vittal's name (Vittal Naam Mukti). He proved it by ascending to heaven with his physical body.

It is said that on the second day of the dark fortnight of Phalgun, in 1650, a Thursday again, Tukaram departed to Vaikuntam (The home of Lord Vishnu) from this place (see picture) in Dehu. He gathered the people around him and took leave from them saying that the time had come for him to leave the world. He called on his devotees to see him on his exit from this world.

Before many astonished devotees, Tukaram was lifted bodily from the banks of the Indrayani River and carried away into space in a flying chariot leading to Vaikunta, the abode of Bhagavan Vishnu. The spot is still seen at Dehu. (See picture with a plaque in Marathi).

Thus, Sant Tukaram suddenly disappeared from this world. However, his devotion and message of love and equality remain eternal and relevant even today, making him a central figure in Indian spirituality.

Chapter - 10
Sant Ramdas

Sant Ramdas, also known as Samarth Ramdas (1608–1681), was a prominent 17th-century Hindu saint, philosopher, and poet from Mahārāshtra. Ramdas was one of the greatest saints of the world. Ramdas was a contemporary of Sant Tukaram and a great devotee of Hanuman and Lord Rama. Most importantly, he inspired Chhatrapati Shivaji Maharaj and served as the prime force behind the establishment of the Maharashtrian Empire.

He was born on the 9th day of the bright fortnight of Chaitra in the year 1608, to Suryajipant and Ranubai Samantha who were Rigvedic Brahmins of Jamadagni lineage. His birth name was Narayan Suryaji Thosar, and he showed early signs of deep spiritual inclination. As a boy, Ramdas acquired some knowledge of Hindu scriptures and developed a liking for meditation and religious study. He was a great devotee of Lord Rama and Hanuman.

The story behind how he came to be called *Ramdas* is linked to his devotion to Lord Rama.

The Wedding Incident

When Narayan was about 12 years old, he was set to marry in accordance with the customs of his family. However, during the wedding ceremony, while the rituals were being performed, Narayan experienced a deep spiritual awakening. He realized that his true calling was not a worldly life, but a life dedicated to God. In a dramatic turn, he left the wedding mandap (ceremonial stage) and renounced worldly life, seeking a higher spiritual purpose.

Dedication to Lord Rama

After leaving the wedding, Narayan wandered as a seeker and devoted himself completely to the worship of Lord Rama. He meditated intensely, and it is said that during one of these meditative states, he received a divine vision of Lord Rama. In that vision, he felt that his life's mission was to serve Rama, and he took on the name Ramdas, meaning "Servant of Rama" (Ram = Lord Rama, das = servant). This moment marked a profound transformation in his life, where his personal identity dissolved into a singular devotion to Lord Rama. From that point on, he lived as Ramdas, dedicating his teachings, life, and mission to spreading the values and ideals of Lord Rama.

Travels and Pilgrimages

Samarth Ramdas traveled extensively travels and established numerous mutts (monasteries) across the Indian subcontinent. He undertook a 12-year pilgrimage, observing social conditions and recording his observations in literary works. He is believed to have traveled to the

Himalayan region during his pilgrimage and reportedly met the sixth Sikh Guru, Guru Hargobind, in Srinagar.

A significant part of his legacy is the establishment of 11 Maruti temples in Mahārāshtra, a pilgrimage route known as the "11 Maruti Yatra." The installation of eleven Maruti Murthis was done from the year 1645 to 1649 AD at the following places:

1. Ram darshan at Chafal and Dasa Maruti
2. Pratapa Maruti
3. Singhanwadi
4. Majgaon
5. Umvraj
6. Masoor
7. Shahapur
8. Bahe Boregaon
9. Shirala
10. Bargaon
11. Manapatle

After his pilgrimage, Ramdas returned to Mahabaleshwar and later established the Samarth sect to unite and spiritually uplift the Hindu population.

Birth of Shivaji

At a time of frequent clashes (16th and 17th centuries) between the Nizam Shahi dynasty of Ahmadnagar and the Adil Shahi dynasty of Bijapur in the Deccan region of India, there emerged a valiant leader by name Shahaji. He married Jeejabai, the daughter of Lakuji Jadhav who was the most influential person within the Ahmadnagar fort. In 1623, his first son was born who was named Sambhaji. On the Shukla Trayodasi day of Phalguni month in the year 1630, Jeejabai delivered another son. As he was born as a gift of Shiva, he was named Shivaji.

Shahaji meets Ramdas

Soon after Shivaji was born, there was a historical meeting between Shahaji and Samarth Ramdas. At this meeting, Shahaji requested Ramdas to take charge as his preceptor and leader and guide him in freeing the country from Muslim rule. Subsequently on many occasions Shahaji consulted Samarth to obtain his advice on several tricky situations.

Shahaji had already brought under his Jagir (area of control), regions of Pune, Junaid, Sangh Mahesh, Triambak and Nasik using Nizam"s name and using his armed forces. Over a period, with blessings from Ramdas, Shivaji displayed his valor and captured many forts that were built by Hindu kings but were later grabbed by Muslim kings and used as tax collection points.

Political Influence.

Ramdas played a crucial role in shaping Shivaji Maharaj's political thought and actions. He encouraged Shivaji to be a just and fair ruler who adhered to ethical values and protected his people. Ramdas believed that spiritual wisdom should be integrated into all aspects of life, including governance and social reform. He encouraged Shivaji to lead a life of dharma (righteousness) and service to the people, which had a lasting impact on the Maratha Empire

Thus, Samarth Ramdas had the unique distinction of not only being a spiritual leader but also a patriotic leader who significantly influenced the political landscape of Mahārāshtra, particularly through his mentorship of Chhatrapati Shivaji Maharaj.

Ramdas's Philosophy of Seva (Service)

The name Ramdas also reflects his philosophy of seva (selfless service). He believed that serving society, upholding righteousness (dharma), and guiding people toward a spiritual life was a way to serve God. This idea of service became central to his teachings, and he worked tirelessly to empower people spiritually and socially through his devotion to Lord Rama. He continuously recited the taaraka mantra "Shree Ram Jai Ram

Jai Jai Ram" while resting beside an idol of Rama brought from Thanjavur in South India.

Thus, the name Ramdas symbolizes his identity as a humble and dedicated servant of Lord Rama, and it became synonymous with his role as a saint, philosopher, and guide to the people of Mahārāshtra.

He is best known for his spiritual teachings, literary works, and influence on Chhatrapati Shivaji Maharaj.

Devotion and Philosophy

Devotion to Lord Rama and Hanuman: Sant Ramdas was an ardent devotee of Lord Rama and Lord Hanuman. His teachings emphasized bhakti (devotion) toward these deities. He believed in the active, dutiful life of Rama rather than a life of renunciation.

Dharma and Self-Discipline: Ramdas taught the importance of moral discipline, self-control, and leading a life aligned with righteousness (dharma). His focus on personal responsibility and social duty had a significant influence on many.

Empowering the Masses: Through his writings and spiritual discourse, he encouraged people to adopt virtues like courage, unity, and dedication, especially during a time when foreign rule had weakened the spirit of the local population.

Literary Works

Sant Ramdas was a prolific writer, and some of his major works include:

Dasbodh: A comprehensive spiritual text written in Marathi, it provides guidance on how to lead a life filled with devotion, wisdom, and discipline. It covers both practical and spiritual aspects of life, offering advice on leadership, duties, and societal ethics.

Dasbodh (दासबोध) consists of 20 Dashakas (also spelled Dasakams), with each Dashakam containing 10 Samas (chapters). Dasbodh is structured as a spiritual and practical guide, blending Advaita Vedanta philosophy with advice on duties, leadership, ethics, and self-discipline.

We share some sample verses from Dasbodh that reveal the amazing teachings of Samarth Ramdas:

आधी प्रपंच करावा नेटका। मग घ्यावें परमार्थविवेका।

येथें आळस करूं नका। विवेकी हो॥

प्रपंच सांडून परमार्थ कराल। तेणें तुम्ही कष्टी व्हाल।

प्रपंच परमार्थ चालवाल। तरी तुम्ही विवेकी॥ -

Dasbodh, dashak 12, samas 1, ovi 1 and 2

Ādhī prapañcha karāvā neṭkā / Mag ghyāvē paramārthavivekā /

Yetheṃ āḷas karūṃ nakā / Vivekī ho //

Prapañcha sāṇḍūn paramārtha karāl / Teṇeṃ tumhī kaṣṭī vhāl /

Prapañcha paramārtha cālavāl / Tarī tumhī vivekī //

Meaning: People should first perform their own respective duties with perfection and then consider practising Spirituality. 'O', intelligent people, do not become lazy. If you try to practice spirituality by neglecting worldly duties, then you will become unhappy. Only when you balance your life and spirituality well will you be considered intellectual.

ऐका स्पृहाची सिकवण। युक्ति बुद्धि शाहाणपण।

जेणें राहे समाधान। निरंतर॥

Aikā spṛhācī sikavaṇa / Yukti buddhi shāhāṇapaṇ /

Jeṇeṃ rāhe samādhān / Nirantar //

This stanza introduces the theme of *nispṛha* (absence of desire/attachment) and sets the tone for the instructions that follow.

> Don't sleep too much but don't remain awake for too long. Never be in the crowd for too long. Never be in the forest for very long too. Don't care too much for the body but don't neglect it to an extent that it disappears. Don't be in the company of the bad. Choose the company of Saints. Don't behave contrary to traditions but don't follow them blindly. Don't love anyone too much but don't be without love. Never be too doubtful.
>
> **SHRI SAMARTH RAMDAS SWAMI MAHARAJ**
>
> *Samas 1 Dashak 14, Dasbodha*

Manache Shlok: These are verses aimed at controlling the mind and guiding it toward a righteous and disciplined life. The verses promote positive thinking, humility, and devotion.

Sundar Kand: It is a Marathi adaptation of the same section from Valmiki Ramayana. This is a revered part of the Ramayana that focuses on the exploits of Lord Hanuman.

The Advaita philosophy of Adi Sankara, the embodiment of Dakshinamurthy, was also taught by Samartha Ramadas.

Influence on Shivaji Maharaj

Sant Ramdas is often remembered for his relationship with Chhatrapati Shivaji Maharaj. He served as a spiritual guide to Shivaji, helping him align his political mission with dharma. Ramdas supported the concept of "Hindavi Swarajya" (self-rule by Hindus) and was an advocate of a just and strong kingdom, which Shivaji sought to establish.

In 1655, Shivaji Maharaj offered his whole kingdom at the feet of his Guru, who in turn placed it in the hands of Lord Rama, symbolizing that the kingdom was meant for divine service, and Shivaji was its caretaker. Ram is a familiar word in Mahārāshtra. I have often heard the rural folks in Mahārāshtra greeting each other with the words, 'Ram, Ram.'

Temples for Hanuman

Ramdas was instrumental in establishing numerous temples dedicated to Lord Hanuman across Mahārāshtra, promoting Hanuman as a symbol of strength, devotion, and service. These temples served as centers of spiritual and social unity. He had also established five Mutts in Thanjavur during his lifetime.

Legacy

Sant Ramdas's legacy lives on in Mahārāshtra through his writings, teachings, and the movements he inspired. His philosophy, emphasizing devotion, discipline, and duty, has had a lasting influence on the spiritual and cultural fabric of the region. His spiritual influence on Shivaji Maharaj also helped shape the Maratha Empire.

Temple at Sajjangad

There is a beautiful temple (see picture) built at Samadhi, the final resting place of Swami Ramadas at Sajjangad, a hilliock near Satara in Mahārāshtra. On the way to the top of the hillock are nine small temples built for Hanuman.

In essence, Sant Ramdas is remembered as a saint who was steadfast in his devotion to Bhagavan Rama. He combined spiritual wisdom with practical action, advocating for both personal growth and societal strength.

The author had the opportunity and privilege to visit Sajjangad, the final resting place of Samarth Ramdas. It was a climb over a hillock. On the way, one can see installations of Hanuman vigrahas (idols). A free lunch is offered to devotees who chant the mantra- "Shri Ram Jaya Ram Jaya Jaya Ram" that reverberates around the hillock. Pictures taken by the author show the Rama temple and the entry at Sajjangad.

Chapter - 11
Sant Chokhamela

Sant Chokhamela was a 14th-century saint and poet from Mahārāshtra, India, who belonged to the Mahar caste, considered an "untouchable" caste at the time. He was a disciple of Namdev and known for his devotion to Lord Vithoba (Panduranga). His Abhangs (sacred poems) are among the earliest examples of Dalit literature that often questioned the discrimination he faced and highlighted the thought that God is beyond caste and social divisions.

Early Life and Caste

Chokhamela was born in the village of Mehuna Raja and later lived in Mangalvedha. He was a Mahar, facing social and religious discrimination due to his caste.

He was attracted by Sant Namdev after he listened to Namdev's songs at Pandharpur. Later he adopted Sant Namdev as his mentor and moved to Pandharpur, the site of the Vithoba temple. A story goes that because of his caste he was not allowed to enter Vithoba's temple at Pandharpur nor was he allowed to even stand at the door and worship. So, in devotional protest he built a hut on the other side of the Chandrabhaga.

Despite the social barriers, Chokhamela developed a deep devotion to Lord Vithoba, often singing and dancing in front of the temple in Pandharpur. Chokhamela and his wife were childless for a long time. They were distressed about it, but it did not deter them from the deep devotion they had to Vittal. With the blessings of Lord Vithoba, they got a son who was named Karmamela. The son too eventually becomes a saint. Despite his strong devotion and the signs of grace from the Lord, Chokhamela was still not permitted to enter the temple. He had to stand at the gate, devotedly praying from a distance.

The Influence of Abhangs

Chokhamela wrote numerous Abhangs, expressing his devotion and challenging the caste system. His Abhangs are considered among the earliest examples of Dalit literature, and his story is celebrated for its message of equality and devotion. Among hundreds of his Abhangs, the most popular and widely sung is "Abir Gulal Udhlit Rang." It is a unique expression of radical self-exploratory poetry in Marathi. He is revered by many as a saint who transcended social barriers through his faith.

Chokhamela's centuries old Abhangs offer a complex and crucial narrative to understand the inception and growth of resistance in future dalit traditions and movements. His Abhangs are significant in the context of the Varkari tradition prevalent in Mahārāshtra. Every year, after the season's first seeds have been sown in farms, devotees travel on foot — a journey called Vari — to the temple dedicated to Vittal or Vithoba. During this trip, devotees sing his Abhangs.

Chokhamela proved devotion to God is not coloured by caste, creed or religion. A true devotee doesn't bother about the mundane world or the behaviour of society towards him. All that a true devotee has is implicit faith in the Supreme power.

The Chokhamela festival is celebrated in Deulgaon Raja to honor his legacy and contribution.

Chapter - 12
Sant Gora Kumbhar

'Kumbhar' means potter. Gora Kumbhar (also known as Goroba) was a potter by profession who turned into a great saint. His father Madhavbua was a great Vitthoba devotee. Believed to have been born in the thirteenth century (Year 1267) at Teradoki in Mahārāshtra, Gora Kumbhar was a contemporary of Sants Namdev and Dnyaneshwar.

Following the footsteps of his father, Gora grew up to be a devotee of Vittal. He carried on his work of making pots but constantly thought of Lord Vitta. Even while working, he expressed his devotion to Lord Vittal by singing bhajans and dancing. There are many stories about Gora Kumbhar, but a poignant incident underscores his deep devotion.

One day, while Kumbhar was mixing clay with his feet, he got immersed in singing and dancing. At that time, his baby son crawled to him. Kumbhar was deeply immersed in thoughts of Vittal paid no attention to the child who got trapped in the clay and died. When his wife found the baby dead, she screamed and blamed Gora for neglect. Gora felt miserable after this tragic incident and went to Pandharpur along with his wife and prayed to Lord Vithal. It is believed that his child was brought back alive due to the divine grace of Lord Vithal.

His story is one of profound devotion, resilience, and the power of faith, even in the face of tragedy. His profession as a potter was a source of spiritual lessons for him. He saw the process of making pots as a metaphor for the purification of the self and the development of a broader perspective in the presence of God.

Gora Kumbhar is known for his Abhangs and his unwavering faith. Gora Kumbhar's story is a testament to the power of devotion and the importance of faith in the face of adversity.

In India, many movies have been produced on the life of Gora Kumbhar. Chakradhari, a Tamil movie was produced in 1948.

He passed away in the year 1317. A temple is dedicated to him in Goraba Ter in Osmanabad district of Mahārāshtra and is visited by numerous devotees.

Chapter - 13
Women Saints of Mahārāshtra

Traditionally, women in the thirteenth century were denied the opportunity for education and going in the spiritual path. However, the rise and growth of the Bhakti movement gave birth to many women saints.

There were many women saints in Mahārāshtra, well-known for their spiritual teachings and devotion. Prominent among them were Janabai and Muktabai.

Sant Janabai was a prominent 13th-century Marathi saint-poet, known for her devotion to Vittal (a form of Krishna) and her role within the Varkari sect. She was a "shudra" (lower caste) woman and worked as a maidservant in the household of Dāmāsheti, the father of Sant Namdev, a prominent Marathi poet-saint. She was a humble and devoted disciple of Namdev.

Janabai's life was marked by unwavering devotion to Vittal. Jana took care of Namdev's family. She was greatly influenced by Namdev's singing and devotion to Lord Vithoba. As a maid servant, she did laborious work including grinding grains, washing clothes, sweeping and cooking. In doing the work she constantly chanted Lord Vithal's name and developed a great devotion to him. It is believed that the Lord used to help her in her daily domestic chores.

Janabai was gifted with poetic talent. She composed numerous Marathi Abhangs making her as one of the most prolific Varkari saints. In one of her poems she appealed to Lord Vithoba, indicating her ambition: "Let me undergo as many births in this world as you please, but grant that my desires are fulfilled. They are that I see Pandharpur and serve Namdev in every birth. I do not mind if I am a bird or a swine, a dog or a cat, but my conditions are that in each of these lives, I must see Pandharpur and serve Namdev. This is the ambition of Namdev's maid."

That sums up the philosophy of Janabai - So intense and sincere was her devotion to Lord Vithoba. There was a movie in Marathi on the life of saint Janabai and her endless devotion for Lord Vithoba.

Muktabai

Muktabai was the younger sister of Saints Dnyaneshwar. Nivritta and Sopan. She was born in 1279 and within a short span of life of about 18 years, she became a renowned saint in the 13th century. She is credited with contributing to the establishment of the Varkari Sampradaya.

Life

Muktabai's early life was harsh as she had faced many struggles within the family and took the burden of a housewife. But her suffering wasn't just social — it was deeply emotional. Her family was often mocked. She bore the mental stress of being a woman in a society that denied her spiritual voice. Yet, she never felt depressed.

Her most famous moment came when the powerful yogi Changdev tried to challenge her brothers with his pride and mystic powers. He arrived on a tiger, with a serpent as a whip.

It wasn't the brothers who humbled him — it was Muktabai, the youngest, who pierced his arrogance with a single verse about humility and love.

"Let your mind melt like wax before the flame of love, or all your power is dust."

Changdev surrendered. Such was the greatnes of Muktabai as a little girl!

Being a sibling of saints, she developed deep devotion to Vittal and started composing devotional poems.

Muktabai's most popular and thoughtful work is said to be a piece titled "ताटी उघडा ज्ञानेश्वरा" (Tati ughada dnyaneshwara) meaning, "Open the door, O Dnyaneshwar." It's also a title of a famous Marathi devotional song and a collection of poems, attributed to Saint Muktabai, who is believed to have spoken to her brother, Saint Dnyaneshwar. The phrase expresses a plea to Dnyaneshwar to open the door of understanding, wisdom, and spiritual enlightenment. It is a nice prayer for knowledge and wisdom, a request for Dnyaneshwar to reveal the truths he knows and to share his wisdom with others.

Muktabai's Samadhi is in Muktainagar (formerly Edlabad), Jalgaon district of Mahārāshtra. It is within the Shree Sant Muktabai Sansthan, a place of worship dedicated to the saint. The temple is considered an ancient shrine, honoring Muktabai as the regional deity.

Chapter - 14
Marathi Abhangs

What is an "Abhang?"

An Abhang (Marathi: अभंग) is a form of devotional poetry and music, deeply rooted in the Bhakti movement of Mahārāshtra. The word 'Bhang' in Marathi means broken. Like in sanskrit, the prefix 'A' refers to the opposite meaning. So the word "Abhang" literally means "unbroken" or "undivided," symbolizing the continuous and unbroken devotion to God that these songs express.

Abhangs are traditionally associated with the 'Varkari sect,' a devotional movement centered around the worship of Vithoba or Vittal, also called Pandurang considered as a form of Lord Vishnu, whose main temple is in Pandharpur, Mahārāshtra. Varkaris are pilgrims who often sing Abhangs, especially during the famous annual pilgrimage, the 'Ashadhi Ekadashi' procession.

What is special about Abhangs?

The composition of Abhangs was done by various saints of Mahārāshtra in different periods. Most of them are based on devotional themes expressing love, yearning, and surrender to the divine Vithoba. They often explore philosophical themes like the futility of worldly desires, the nature of true devotion, moral living and humility.

Unlike the classical Sanskrit hymns, Abhangs are composed primarily written and sung in Marathi. The lyrics are simple, straightforward and often imbued with rich metaphors and symbols, making complex spiritual concepts relatable to ordinary devotees.

Abhangs are typically sung during as kirtans (devotional singing sessions) and bhajans (devotional group singing), especially during the

Varkari pilgrimages to Pandharpur. The songs are often accompanied by instruments like the tabla, harmonium, and cymbals, creating a rhythmic and uplifting musical experience. The repetitive nature of the songs helps to induce a meditative state, allowing singers and listeners to focus on the divine and experience a sense of spiritual immersion.

In contrast to bhajans, which are meditative, Abhangs evoke a feeling of communal ecstasy.

We share a few famous Abhangs in Marathi from well-known Sant Tukaram and Sant Dnyaneshwar, along with their transliterations and meanings. These Abhangs are deeply spiritual and convey different aspects of devotion, morality, and surrender to God.

A very simple Abhang is "*Vittal Vittal Jay Hari Vittal*" by Sant Tukaram.

This is one of the most famous and frequently sung Abhangs in bhajans.

विठ्ठल विठ्ठल जय हरी विठ्ठल

विठ्ठल विठ्ठल जय हरी विठ्ठल

Vittal! Vittal! Victory to Lord Vittal!

Vittal! Vittal! Victory to Lord Vittal!

Why repeat the same name? The continuous repetition of Vittal's name is a form of 'nama-smarana' (constant remembrance of the name), which is believed to lead to liberation. The focus is on 'complete surrender to the divine' through the joyful, repetitive chanting of Vittal's name.

Again, Sant Tukaram sings:

समचरण दृष्टि विटेवरी साजिरी। तेथे माझी हरी वृत्ती राहो ||१||

आणिक न लगे मायिक पदार्थ। तेथे माझे आर्त नको देवा ||२||

ब्रह्मादिक पदे दुःखाची शिराणी। तेथे दुश्चित झणी जडो देसी ||३||

तुका म्हणे त्याचे कळले आम्हा वर्म। जे जे कर्मधर्म नाशवंत ||४||

Transliteration:

Samacharan drushti vitewari sajiri, tethe mazi Hari vrutti raaho...1

Aanik na lage maayik padartha, tethe maze aart nako deva...2

Brahmadik pade dukkhaachi shiranee, tethe duschitta zanee jado desee...3

Tuka mhane tyaache kalale aamha Varma, je je karmadharma naashvant...4

Roughly translated, the meaning of this Abhang is like:

1. Oh Hari! May my mind always be attached to those feet of the Lord Vithal, which are on the brick. The gaze of the eyes, too, is constantly engaged on the feet.

2. I do not want any material things that are seen by my eyes, which in reality, have no existence. Lord may my mind never get attached to these things!

3. Brahmalok (planetary systems) all ultimately lead to sorrow and hence may my heart never get attached to them.

4. Tukaram says, I have understood the secret of all the karmas and dharmas. They are all temporary, that will eventually perish.

One more of Tukaram's Abhang:

काये करूनि करी धंदा । चित्त गोविंदा तुझे पायी ॥ १ ॥

ऐसा संकल्पाचे संधी । माझे बुद्धी धीर द्यावा ॥ २ ॥

Kāye karūni karī dhanda | Chitta Govindā tujhe pāyī || 1 ||

Let the body engage in worldly work or business; but let the mind remain at your feet, O Govinda (Krishna).

Aisā sankalpāche sandhī | Mājhe buddhī dhīr dyāvā || 2 ||

Grant my intellect the strength and steadiness to hold firmly to this resolve.

कुटुंबाचा तुम्हा भार । मज व्यवहार निमित्त ॥ ३ ॥

तुका म्हणे करिता काम । हृदयी नाम धरीन मीं ॥ ४ ॥

Kuṭumbāchā tumhā bhār | Maj vyavahār nimitta || 3 ||

The burden of the family is truly Yours; I am merely the instrument in these worldly affairs.

Tukā mhaṇe karitā kām | Hṛdayī nām dharīn mī || 4 ||

Tuka says: While I perform my duties, I will keep Your name ever in my heart.

Meaning of the Abhang:

Sant Tukaram says, "Even as I perform my duties in the world, my heart and mind should always be devoted to God." This reflects *'karma-yoga'*— action without attachment, with a God-centered mind. He prays for mental clarity and determination, asking God to help him stay committed to this balance of action and devotion. He surrenders all responsibilities to God, saying, "You take care of my family; I'm just a means You are using." This shows humility and surrender of ego. Even during work, Tukaram resolves to keep God's name in his heart, showing how spiritual life can be lived even while engaging with the world.

It is relevant to quote a verse from Chapter 11 of the *Bhagavad Gita*:

मत्कर्मकृन्मत्परमो मद्भक्तः सङ्गवर्जितः ।
निर्वैरः सर्वभूतेषु यः स मामेति पाण्डव ॥ ११-५५॥

mat-karma-kṛn mat-paramo mad-bhaktaḥ saṅga-varjitaḥ
nirvairaḥ sarva-bhūteṣhu yaḥ sa mām eti pāṇḍava

"He who performs all actions for My sake, who looks upon Me as the supreme goal, who is devoted to Me, free from attachment and without enmity toward any being — such a person, O Pandava, comes to Me." (11.55)

Saint Tukaram beautifully conveys the essence of this verse in simple, accessible words.

In the very first line of one of his *Abhangas* (devotional verses), he makes it clear that one need not renounce worldly duties to attain spiritual growth. What truly matters is a transformation in one's mental attitude.

If a person claims, *"I am the doer; I accomplished this or that,"* they take ownership of their actions. With this sense of doership comes an expectation of results. When outcomes align with our desires, we feel joy; when they do not, we feel sorrow, disappointment, or even despair.

Thus, we experience happiness or suffering based on the consequences of actions we perceive as our own. Tukaram emphasizes that liberation lies not in abandoning action, but in surrendering the ego and cultivating devotion, detachment, and equanimity.

Turning to Sant Dyaneshwar, he sings the following Abhang:

रुप पाहतां लोचनीं । सुख जालें वो साजणी ॥१॥
तो हा विठ्ठल बरवा । तो हा माधव बरवा ॥ध्रु०॥
बहुता सकृतांची जोडी । म्हणुनि विठ्ठलीं आवडी ॥२॥
सर्व सुखाचें आगरु । बापरखुमादेविवरु ॥३॥

Transliteration and meaning:

Rūpa pāhatāṁ lōcanīṁ. Sukha jālēṁ vō sājaṇī.

Seeing the beauty (beautiful form) by my eyes, I got the bliss… o friend

Tō hā viṭhṭhala baravā. Tō hā mādhava baravā.

That one Vittal is beautiful, that one Madhava is beautiful

Bahutāṁ sukr̥tāñcī jōḍī. Mhaṇuni viṭhṭhalīṁ āvaḍī.

Multiplying the good deeds, (then only) thus starts the love for Vittal

Sarva sukhācēṁ āgara. Bāpa rakhumādēvīvarū.

Home of all the bliss, (is) father Rakhuma Devi's (Rukmini's) husband [referring to Vittal].

Another Abhang by Sant Dnyaneshwar.

This is an exquisite Abhang that speaks about the unity of the soul with God.

अवघा रंग एक झाला, आनंदाची जाणीव झाली ||

विसरली देहभान, राहिले फकत नाम ||

अवघा रंग एक झाला ||

Avghā raṅg ek jhālā, ānandāchī jāṇīv jhālī ||

Visaralī dehabhān, rāhilē phakta nām ||

Avghā raṅg ek jhālā ||

Meaning:

All the colors have become one, a realization of divine bliss has emerged.

I have forgotten the awareness of my body, only the name (of God) remains.

All the colors have become one.

In this Abhang, Sant Dnyaneshwar beautifully expresses the state of spiritual unity with God. The "colors becoming one" symbolizes the merging of the individual soul (the devotee) with the divine (God). In this state of oneness, the ego and bodily identity are forgotten, leaving only the pure consciousness of God's name. This reflects the goal of Bhakti: merging into the divine through devotion.

Sant Eknath sings, "Rama Krishna Hari" - a popular Abhang that reflects on God's different forms and names.

राम कृष्ण हरी, राम कृष्ण हरी,

राम कृष्ण हरी, राम कृष्ण हरी!

Rama, Krishna, Hari (Vishnu),

Rama, Krishna, Hari!

This simple yet profound Abhang emphasizes the unity of Vishnu's different forms — Rama, Krishna, and Hari. Sant Eknath teaches that chanting the names of God, regardless of which form one chooses to worship, leads to spiritual liberation. The repetition of God's names is a central practice in Bhakti and is believed to purify the heart and bring peace.

Musical Style of Abhangs

Abhangs have a distinctive musical style that is deeply connected to devotional group singing in the Bhakti tradition of Mahārāshtra. The musical structure of Abhangs is simple yet spiritually profound, designed to evoke devotion and create a collective spiritual atmosphere during religious gatherings, pilgrimages, and temple rituals.

The key elements of the musical style of Abhangs include:

- **Rhythmic and Repetitive Structure**

Repetition is one of the core characteristics of Abhangs, both lyrically and musically. The repetitive chanting of the name Vittal creates a meditative and rhythmic pattern that helps the singer and listeners enter into a devotional state. The structure often follows a pattern where a lead singer (called a 'keertankar') sings a verse, and the chorus or group repeats it, reinforcing the spiritual message.

- **Melodic Simplicity**

The melody of Abhangs is generally simple and easy to follow, allowing everyone to join in. Since these are songs of the common people, the tunes are often straightforward and folk-like, which makes them easy to sing even without formal musical training. Although simple, the melodies are emotionally rich, meant to inspire devotion and connect the singer with the divine.

- **Ragas (Melodic Framework)**

While Abhangs are primarily folk songs in nature, many of them have been adapted into Hindustani classical music. Classical singers often sing Abhangs tuned to ragas -the melodic frameworks used in Indian classical music.

Ragas like Bhairavi, Yaman, Bhimpalasi, and Malkauns are frequently used to render Abhangs, depending on the mood and time of the performance. For example, Raga Bhairavi is often used for devotional or closing pieces in Indian classical concerts. Even when set in a classical raga, the focus remains on bhakti (devotion) rather than technical virtuosity.

- **Talas (Rhythmic Cycles)**

Abhangs usually follow a simple tala (rhythmic cycle), like Keherwa (8 beats) or Dadra (6 beats), which provides a steady, lively rhythm to the singing. The repetitive rhythm keeps the mood upbeat and energetic, helping to maintain the momentum of the performance during long sessions of devotional singing. In traditional temple or pilgrimage settings, the rhythmic clapping of the devotees often accompanies percussion, further enhancing the communal aspect of the music.

Instruments Used in Abhangs

Abhang performances are accompanied by traditional instruments that add to the energy and devotional fervor. The instruments include:

- **Mridangam or Pakhawaj:** These double-headed drums provide the primary rhythm in Abhang performances.
- **Tabla:** A more classical Indian drum that is often used in Abhang performances that have a classical or semi-classical feel.
- **Harmonium:** This small hand-pumped reed organ provides the melodic base. The harmonium usually plays the melody in sync with the singer and is a central instrument in Abhang performances.
- **Cymbals (Taal or Jhanj):** Small handheld cymbals that maintain the rhythmic pace. They add a metallic, sharp sound to the

performance, helping the rhythm cut through the layers of melody and vocals.

- **Tanpura:** A string instrument used to provide a continuous drone in the background, helping to create a steady, stable, meditative sound environment.

Cultural and Musical Impact

Abhangs are a central feature of the annual Varkari pilgrimages to Pandharpur, where devotees walk for hundreds of kilometers, singing these songs in groups. The rhythmic and repetitive nature of Abhangs helps create a sense of unity and collective devotion.

During festivals like "Ashadhi Ekadashi" which is one of the most important events for the Varkaris, Abhangs are sung by groups throughout the day and night, adding to the spiritual atmosphere of the event.

Abhangs have transcended their religious origins and have become a part of Mahārāshtra's cultural identity. Even today, they are sung by classical and folk musicians, and many have been adapted into modern music.

Abhangs that are performed in the Hindustani classical style, blend devotional themes with classical music's technical precision and depth. This has allowed the genre to gain a new audience, while still maintaining its roots in devotional practice. Legendary classical singers like Pandit Bhimsen Joshi and Lata Mangeshkar have rendered famous Abhangs, further popularizing this devotional genre across India.

Spiritual and Emotional Experience

Devotees find the spiritual experience of singing or listening to an Abhang to be very powerful. The repetition of Vithal's name in the songs is said to create an emotional connection with the divine, while the simplicity and beauty of the lyrics make the songs easy for everyone to participate in, regardless of their social or educational background

For many Varkaris and devotees, Abhangs are more than just songs; they are a form of living devotion, where singing becomes an act of worship and a path to divine grace.

Abhangs carry deep spiritual wisdom while maintaining a direct, heartfelt expression of devotion. They combine poetic beauty with simple language, making them accessible to people of all backgrounds, while offering profound insights into surrender, love, and the pursuit of God. Whether through emotional longing, the simplicity of daily devotion, or the joy of unity with the divine, these Abhangs reflect the essence of Bhakti.

In a nutshell, Abhangs are not only a musical tradition but also a deep expression of personal devotion and community worship. Their influence has endured for centuries, providing a spiritual and cultural lifeline to millions of Hindus, both in Mahārāshtra and beyond. Abhangs have the unique ability to attract even a passerby to sing along. Through their rhythmic melodies, heartfelt lyrics, and connection to the divine, Abhangs have become a key part of the spiritual landscape of India.

Chapter - 15
The Varkari Tradition

The Varkari Tradition is an annual religious pilgrimage that holds immense spiritual significance in the state of Mahārāshtra. The key feature of the Varkari tradition is a deep devotional movement centered around the worship of Vithoba (also known as Vittal), a form of Lord Vishnu at the Temple in Pandharpur. The annual event takes place on the auspicious day of 'Ashadhi Ekadashi,' typically in June or July. The pilgrimage to Pandharpur is called Wari, and the devotees who undertake this journey are known as Varkaris. The Pandharpur Wari is more than a journey; it's a living testament to Mahārāshtra's deep-rooted spiritual and cultural heritage. As millions walk the sacred paths to honour Lord Vithoba, they engage in a collective act of devotion that transcends centuries.

Palki Procession

The tradition includes a Palki procession that refers to the ceremonial carrying of palkis (palanquins) holding the sacred padukas (footwear) of the saints of the Bhakti tradition. These relics are generally carried from Alandi, Dehu and the saints' hometowns to the Vithoba temple in Pandharpur. The processions for two of the popular saints - Sant Dnyaneshwar and Sant Tukaram-are the largest and famous:

1. **Sant Dnyaneshwar Palki:** Begins at Alandi, near Pune, the town where Sant Dnyaneshwar took samadhi (left his mortal body).

2. **Sant Tukaram Palki:** Begins at Dehu, near Pune, where Sant Tukaram lived and preached.

The Palki carries the padukas of the saints in a decorated palanquin, accompanied by thousands of Varkari devotees who walk together all the way to Pandharpur, singing Abhangs and chanting the name of Lord Vittal.

The palki is highly decorated, often adorned with flowers and saffron cloth. Special prayers are offered at various stops along the way, where the palki halts, and the devotees gather to pay their respects to the relics.

Most pilgrims are dressed in traditional attire (men wear dhoti, kurta and headgear and women wear nine-yard saree in Maharashtrian style). They travel on foot, walking for about 15–20 days across the scenic hilly landscape of Mahārāshtra. The procession follows a traditional route, passing through several villages and towns, where locals welcome the Varkaris with food, shelter, and water.

Devotional Spirit

The colourful Varkari procession is characterized by the deep spiritual devotion and humility of the participants. Most Varkaris walk barefoot singing Abhangs in the most cheerful moods. Some of them dance on the streets in ecstasy.

Bhajan Singing by Varkaris

Source: Creative Commons

The chanting of "Vittal Vittal" and "Gyanba Tukaram" (referring to Sant Dnyaneshwar and Sant Tukaram) reverberates throughout the journey, creating a devotional atmosphere.

The Varkaris generally wear simple white clothes and caps, and a tilak on their foreheads. Many of them wear garland made of tulsi (basil) beads around their necks. Their devotion is marked by a commitment to a life of service, devotion, and communal harmony. Many pilgrims carry saffron-colored flags, symbolizing their spiritual mission. The long march is often seen as a vibrant sea of devotion.

Ashadhi Ekadashi

The culmination of the pilgrimage occurs on Ashadhi Ekadashi, a significant auspicious day in the Hindu calendar that falls in the month of Ashadha (June–July). This day is dedicated to Lord Vishnu, and in Mahārāshtra, it is associated specifically with the worship of Vithoba.

Significance of Ashadhi Ekadashi

According to Hinduism, Lord Vishnu stays over the cosmic ocean of milk called Ksheersagar in Sanskrit. He reclines on a coiled serpent called Adi Shesha. It is believed that Vishnu foes to sleep on the Ashadi Ekadashi day-also called Shayani Ekadashi. It is said that Lord Vishnu wakes up from his slumber awakens four months later Prabodhini Ekadashi - eleventh day of bright fortnight in the Hindu month Kartik (October-November). This period is known as Chaturmas (four months) and coincides with the rainy season. So, Ashadhi Ekadashi is celebrated on a grand scale by worshipping Pandurang - an incarnation of Lord Vishnu. On this occasion, devotees traditionally observe fast and spend the entire night singing prayers.

The Palkis carrying the padukas of saints arrive in Pandharpur just before Ashadhi Ekadashi, and the devotees offer prayers and participate in the grand celebrations held at the Vithoba temple.

Ancient Tradition

The Varkari tradition dates to the 13th century and is associated with the Bhakti movement, a spiritual renaissance in India that emphasized personal devotion over ritualistic worship. The saints of Mahārāshtra, like Sant Dnyaneshwar, Sant Tukaram, Sant Namdev, Sant Eknath, and others, preached a message of equality, devotion, and love for God. The Varkari Tradition is a symbol of that devotion. It emphasizes a simple controlled approach to life, moral behavior, and devotion. They practice vegetarianism, avoid alcohol and tobacco, and follow a strict lacto-vegetarian diet.

Main features of this ancient tradition include:

1. **Worship of Vithoba:** Varkaris venerate Vithoba, as the central focus of their devotion.

2. **Pilgrimage to Pandharpur:** The annual pilgrimage, known as the Pandharpur Wari, is an ancient traditional practice. Varkaris travel on foot to Pandharpur, carrying palkhis (palanquins) of saints' footprints.

3. **Traditional Dress:** It is typically a dhoti (unstitched long piece of white cloth) and an upper garment (kurta) for men, often with a pheta (turban) or a white cap. Most carry a tulasi mala (rosary made from tulsi wood). Women often wear a long nine-yard saree, also known as a Nauvari saree, in a distinctive Maharashtrian style.

4. **Emphasis on Moral Behavior:** The Varkari tradition stresses ethical conduct, emphasizing values like respect for others, forgiveness, non-violence, love, and humility.

5. **Food:** and Dietary Practices: Varkaris typically follow a vegetarian diet, some excluding onion and garlic, and observe fasting on Ekadashi days (twice a month).

6. **Simplicity and Humility:** The Varkari way of life emphasizes simplicity, both in attire and lifestyle, symbolizing their devotion and humility.

7. **Social Equality:** The tradition promotes social equality, rejecting discrimination based on caste or social status.

8. **Bhajans and Kirtans:** Varkaris sing Abhangs, in praise of Vithoba, often accompanied by musical instruments.

9. **Dindi Tradition:** Varkaris travel in groups called Dindis, which are processions carrying the palkhis.

10. **Importance of the Vari:** The annual pilgrimage to Pandharpur is a significant event for Varkaris, who dedicate themselves to the journey and the spiritual experience it offers.

Today, the Pandharpur Wari attracts millions of pilgrims each year. People from all walks of life — rich and poor, rural and urban, old and young — join the Palki procession, walking together in an act of collective devotion.

The journey to Pandharpur in the Varkari tradition is physically demanding. However, most devotees see it as a "spiritual purification" and an act of penance, where devotees can surrender their ego and connect with God.

The tradition, which spans centuries, continues to thrive in the modern world, drawing more participants every year, making it a living testament to the enduring power of Bhakti.

Chapter - 16
Reverence for Saints

Many people, particularly from the Western world, often ask this question:

How has the deep reverence for saints — many of whom were seemingly ordinary individuals by worldly standards — continued for thousands of years in India?

The answer lies in the foundational principles of Hindu thought and culture, which offer a different lens for recognizing greatness and achievement.

1. Greatness Is Defined by Inner Realization, Not Outer Accomplishment

In modern society, greatness is typically associated with scientific discoveries, material success, or political influence. However, in Hinduism, true greatness lies in inner realization — mastery over the mind, selfless living, and spiritual awakening.

Saints may not have invented material tools or technologies, but they accessed eternal truths and profoundly transformed the lives of others. Their legacy is not measured in wealth or accolades, but in the timeless wisdom and peace they radiated.

2. Living Examples of Dharma (Righteousness)

Many saints led humble, even obscure lives, yet became paragons of dharma — embodying truth, devotion, compassion, and detachment.

For instance:

- **Sant Eknath**, though a low-paid government clerk, is venerated for his unwavering integrity and devotion.
- **Sant Namdev**, a tailor by caste, is celebrated for his devotional poetry, still sung with deep emotion today.

These individuals conquered inner enemies — ego, fear, and desire — in ways that no external science can.

3. Spiritual Achievement as the Highest Goal

While science explores the external universe, saints explored the **inner cosmos** — the workings of the mind, the nature of consciousness, and the path to liberation.

They offered powerful tools for transformation:

- **Mantras**
- **Meditation**
- **Satsangh** (company of the wise)
- **Vairagya** (detachment from material cravings)

This is the science of the soul, whose fruits are peace, clarity, moral strength, and transcendence — real, if not always quantifiable.

4. Embodiments of Peace and Grace

Saints are believed to radiate **shanti** (peace) and **kripa** (grace), not merely through teachings, but through their presence. This is why their places of worship and meditation — samadhis and temples — continue to uplift people centuries later. Even modern visitors, including many from the West, report a sense of serenity and transformation.

5. Spiritual Anchors in a Turbulent World

In times of social upheaval or personal struggle, saints offer ethical and spiritual grounding. They become symbols of timeless values in a world often governed by ego, materialism, and conflict. Their lives remind us of what really matters.

6. Moral Aspiration Through Reverence

Reverence for saints often inspires moral striving. People think: *If Sant Tukaram could remain honest and humble through immense hardship, why can't I?*

In this sense, devotion becomes a **source of inner motivation**, not blind worship. It is not about idolizing the person but about aspiring toward their virtues.

A Modern Analogy

To understand this in familiar terms: Think of saints as the Einsteins of consciousness or the Mahatmas of moral courage. Just as we honor scientific geniuses for mapping the physical universe, saints are revered in India for charting the vast, intricate universe within.

Saints like Tukaram, Dnyaneshwar, Chokhamela, and others made people believe that God resides in everything: living and non-living, high and low. They didn't just preach scripture – They embodied it!

This idea of God's nearness to man, and His ever readiness to come to their help, runs through all the Bhakti literature of the Maharashtrian saints. Most of these saints believed in the reality of Puranic stories that portray Bhagavan as 'Aapatbhandava' - a friend in need" or "protector in times of trouble"

In conclusion, Maharashtrian saints are still being revered in modern times because they preached a message of love, equality, and devotion that resonated with people across different social strata. Their teachings, often conveyed through accessible Marathi language, emphasized personal connection with the divine, transcended caste and religious barriers, and promoted social reform.

Chapter - 17
The Echoes of Devotion

The echoes of devotion spread far and wide from Mahārāshtra. They created a profound and far-reaching impact — spiritually, socially, and culturally — on other parts of India historically, and more recently, on a global scale. The saints' teachings, devotional practices, and inclusive philosophies have transcended regional boundaries and found relevance in diverse contexts.

Impact on Southern India

Several Maharashtrian saints, especially from the Bhakti movement, have influenced devotional traditions in Southern India. Sant Namdev is known to have traveled extensively throughout India, including South India, alongside the sage Jnanadev, spreading their message of devotion and unity.

The early Bhakti saints in South India came from diverse social backgrounds – from the wealthy and nobles to peasants and untouchables – yet they shared a common faith of pure devotion to a personal God surpassing ritual status or caste. Many kings of the Pallava and Chola dynasties patronized these devotional movements, thus nurturing Bhakti ideals into South Indian culture. By the early medieval era, the cults of Vishnu and Shiva in the South had been greatly influenced by the Alvars and Nayanmars who were key Tamil saints in the Bhakti movement in South India, particularly between the 6th and 11th centuries. The Alvars were devotees of Lord Vishnu, while the Nayanmars were devoted to Lord Shiva. They both composed devotional hymns and played a significant role in popularizing Bhakti, a form of personal, intense devotion to a deity, across various social strata.

In Karnataka, during the 15th–16th centuries, Purandara Dasa and Kanaka Dasa were prominent Haridasa saints who composed devotional songs in Kannada focusing on Vishnu (Krishna). Purandara Dasa's Kirtans not only spread devotion but also laid the foundations of South Indian classical music. The Haridasa movement led by saints like Purandara Dasa (1484-1565) and Kanaka Dasa (1509-1609) was partly influenced by Marathi Bhakti traditions. They shared the Bhakti ideology and adopted it in their Kirtans crossing linguistic and regional borders.

The Dakshina Bharatha Sampradaya Bhajan tradition, also known as the South Indian Sampradaya Bhajan tradition, is attributed to a trinity of figures who lived between 1684 and 1817, according to Madras Heritage and Carnatic Music. This trinity included Sri Bhagavan Nama Bhodendra Saraswathi Swamigal (17th-century Hindu pontiff and the 59th Jagathguru of the Kanchi Mutt), Sridhara Venkatesa Ayyaval (1635-1720), and Marudanallur Sadhguru Swamigal (1777-1817). While Ayyaval is considered the father of this Bhajan tradition, Bhodendra Saraswathi formalized the rules and methods of conducting Bhajans. Sadguru Swamigal, who lived much later, traveled widely picking up many additions to the Bhajans. He refined the tradition with a systematic rendering of 'Nama Samkeertanam' including devotional songs gathered from different parts of India. Today, the Marathi Abhangs are an essential part of the South Indian Sampradaya Bhajan.

While it may not be entirely accurate to say that the Maharashtrian Bhajan tradition was a direct forerunner of the Sampradaya Bhajan tradition, there is a definite cross-cultural exchange between the two, especially through the Bhakti movement that connected various parts of India.

Both the Maharashtrian and South Indian Bhakti traditions emphasized personal devotion, love for God, and social equality, albeit expressed in different regional languages and cultural contexts.

Bhakti movement in Eastern India

By the late 15th and early 16th century, Bhakti fervor had reached Eastern India. In Bengal, the charismatic saint Chaitanya Mahaprabhu (1486–1534) led a renaissance of Krishna devotion. Chaitanya taught love for Radha and Krishna as the highest truth, often entering ecstatic trances while chanting God's names. He and his companions (the Six Goswamis of Vrindavan) organized sankirtana – congregational singing and dancing in praise of Krishna – as a joyful, communal form of worship. Chaitanya's movement (Gaudiya Vaishnavism) made devotional music and dance a central spiritual practice and attracted people across social divisions. His emphasis on hari-nama (chanting the holy names) and universal love left a lasting mark; even today, Bengali culture's spiritual core is enriched by devotional songs like the Baul folk tunes and the annual celebration of Krishna (Rasa Lila) inspired by Chaitanya's teachings.

Bhakti spreads in Western India

Gujarat's Bhakti landscape was shaped by saints who expressed devotion in the Gujarati language and local folk culture. A foremost figure is Narsinh Mehta (15th century), a poet who sang heartfelt bhajans to Lord Krishna. Narsinh Mehta's famous composition "Vaishnava Jana To" ("One who is a devotee of Vishnu…") extols ethical living and empathy; centuries later, it was revered by Mahatma Gandhi as an anthem of compassion. Through such songs, Narsinh preached that true devotion lies in seeing God in every being, again reinforcing Bhakti's egalitarian ethos. Gujarat also had the influence of the Pushtimarg (Path of Grace) sect founded by Vallabhacharya, which centered on Krishna's child form and seva (loving service) rather than renunciation.

Bhakti in Northern India

Northern India witnessed a vibrant tapestry of Bhakti movements between the 15th and 17th centuries, producing some of the most renowned saint-poets. A distinctive feature in the north was the rise of the Sant tradition – mystic poets who often spoke of a formless God (Nirguna Brahman) and criticized religious orthodoxy. Among them, the saint Kabir, from the weaver community (c. 15th c.) stands out as a key leader. Kabir composed couplets (dohas) that pierced through communal divisions – he chastised both Hindu temple-goers and Muslim mullahs if they lacked true devotion, proclaiming the unity of God beyond labels. In one famous verse he wrote, "दुनिया बड़ी ख़िलाफ़ है", implying that worldly divisions mean nothing since "God is within". His poems, full of earthy metaphors, taught that only bhakti (devotion) and prem (love) can reveal God, not empty rituals. Kabir's egalitarian theology (influenced by both Hindu Bhakti and Sufi Islam) resonated widely – remarkably, his verses are included in the Sikh scripture, the Guru Granth Sahib, showing the cross-fertilization of devotional ideas.

Surdas (16th c.), a blind poet, sang hundreds of songs for baby Krishna in Braj language, detailing Krishna's divine play (leelas) and thus enriching the Krishna bhakti tradition of Vrindavan. Mirabai wandered through the north (Vrindavan, Brindaban) singing to Krishna with abandon. Other notable northern saints include Ravidas (a Dalit cobbler saint and disciple of Ramananda, whose songs of a casteless devotion inspired many), Namdev of Mahārāshtra who traveled north, and Dadu Dayal of Rajasthan. Despite differences – some worshipped Rama or Krishna, others a formless God – these saints collectively conveyed a message of love, humility, and inner realization. Their verses in vernacular Hindi, Braj, or Punjabi democratized spiritual knowledge. Indeed, by the end of the 17th century, the Bhakti movement had created a rich mosaic of devotional literature and practice across North India, uniting people beyond sectarian lines through the simple act of singing the name of God.

Overall Impact in India

Many Bhakti leaders themselves came from marginalized communities – for instance, Kabir was from a low-caste weaver family, Ravidas was an "untouchable" cobbler, Chokhamela inMahārāshtra was from the Dalit Mahar caste, and women like Mirabai (a princess) or Akkamahadevi (a Kannada Sharana saint) boldly stepped into the role of spiritual giants. These examples provided a powerful social message of inclusion. Women and lower castes found a voice in Bhakti, as the movement allowed them to become revered figures and to participate in devotional gatherings on an equal footing.

Contemporary Global Impact

In recent decades, the spiritual and philosophical contributions of these saints have gained recognition globally:

The 'International Society for Krishna Consciousness (ISKCON)' and other global bhakti movements have adopted and popularized Marathi Abhangs, kirtan practices and the philosophies of saints like Tukaram and Dnyaneshwar.

We also witness the surge in the growth Yoga communities and spiritual seekers worldwide who now engage in chanting and devotional singing inspired by these saints.

Literary works like the 'Dnyaneshwari' (a Marathi commentary on the Bhagavad Gita by Sant Dnyaneshwar) have been translated into several languages and studied in academic circles around the world. Sant Tukaram's abhangs, translated into English, have drawn interest for their poetic beauty and philosophical depth.

Diaspora and Cultural Festivals

The Maharashtrian diaspora in the USA, UK, Canada, and Australia actively celebrate Ashadhi Ekadashi, Tukaram Beej, and Namdev Jayanti, introducing these traditions to broader communities around the globe. Varkari-style pilgrimages and devotional gatherings (such as kirtan melas) are held in Western countries, attracting spiritual practitioners from diverse backgrounds.

Thus, the saints of Mahārāshtra, have left an enduring legacy that has crossed linguistic, regional, and now international boundaries. Their message — centered on love, devotion, humility, and social equality — continues to inspire spiritual seekers, scholars, musicians, and reformers around the world. The global relevance of their teachings today reflects not only their spiritual power but also their timeless impact on humanity. Today, the echoes of devotion from India can be heard in most parts of the world.

Chapter - 18
The Modern-Era Mahāns

The modern-era Mahāns of Mahārāshtra are revered figures from the 18th century onwards, known for their profound spiritual influence, social reform, or saintly lives. While classical saints like Sant Dnyaneshwar and Sant Tukaram belonged to the medieval Bhakti movement, these modern-era Mahāns carried that legacy into newer context sometimes blending it with mysticism, service, or reform.

In this chapter, we describe some of the most recognized modern-era Mahāns of Mahārāshtra, their contributions, and places associated with them:

1. Shri Swami Samarth of Akkalkot (1800–1878)

Considered an incarnation of Lord Dattatreya, Swami Samarth lived in Akkalkot (Solapur district of Mahārāshtra). His origins are not clearly known. He is believed to have arrived at Akkalkot around the year 1856 where he lived for 22 years. He was a contemporary of another Mahān, Manik Prabhu (described later). Swami Samarth regarded Manik Prabhu as a brother.

It is believed that he became the preceptor of many great souls like Ramakrishna ParaMahānsa, Sai Baba of Shirdi, Shankar Maharaj, and Gajajan Maharaj of Shegaon. So, He is revered as the teacher of many spiritual teachers i.e. guru of gurus.

He was well-known for curing illnesses, guiding devotees, and practicing fierce but compassionate spiritual guidance. He attained samadhi in Akkalkot, Mahārāshtra where there is well-maintained temple & samadhi shrine, easily accessible from Solapur by road/rail.

2. Gajanan Maharaj of Shegaon (1878–1910)

Gajanan Maharaj is believed to have appeared mysteriously in Shegaon, a small town in Vidarbha, sometime in the year 1878. His arrival in the village was followed by many divine events. Over the years, he performed countless miracles, healed the sick, and offered profound spiritual wisdom to his followers. His teachings, grounded in devotion and righteousness, created an unbreakable bond between him and his followers.

There are very few of his spoken words, most of his communication was through actions and blessings. In a short span of 32 years, he influenced the lives of numerous people with his spiritual knowledge and power. He performed miracles, inspired devotion and service, especially Annadan (free food).

At his final resting place in Shegaon, a Samadhi Temple has been built in marble stones. This is a beautiful temple built in memory of Gajanan Maharaj. This temple is a magnificent blend of traditional and modern architectural styles. Right at the center of the temple is the Samadhi Mandir, where Gajanan Maharaj's resting place lies, in a serene and spiritually charged environment. This sacred spot draws pilgrims seeking peace and divine intervention. Adjacent to Samadhi is the Shri Ram Mandir, where Lord Ram, Goddess Sita, and Lord Lakshman are enshrined. The temple complex also features the Sabha Mandap, a grand hall adorned with intricately carved depictions of the saint's life and miracles. These beautiful carvings serve to describe the saint's story, connecting visitors with the divine acts that shaped his legacy.

Shegaon is in Buldhana district located about 16 kms from NH-6 (Via-Khamgaon). Nearest airports are Nagpur and Aurangabad at a driving distance of about 5 hours. There is also a Shegaon rail station of central railway located on the Mumbai- Nagpur track.

Readers can get more details of Gajanan Maharaj at https://www.gajananmaharaj.org/.

3. Shirdi Sai Baba (1838–1918)

Shirdi Sai Baba's early years are a mystery. Most accounts mention his birth as a Hindu Brahmin and his subsequent adoption by a Sufi fakir, a Muslim mendicant. Later in life he claimed to have had a Hindu guru.

It is believed that Sai Baba arrived in Shirdi, in the western Indian state of Mahārāshtra, about the year 1858 and remained there until his death in 1918.

Shirdi Sai Baba and Shri Gajanan Maharaj were contemporaries and knew each other.

Sai Baba's teachings often took the form of paradoxical parables and displayed both his disdain for the rigid formalism.

Sai Baba is said to have performed many miracles that were witnessed by the public. One of them was that he lit lamps with water as the grocer merchant refused to sell oil to Baba without money.

He would often predict the unspoken questions of devotees by reading their minds. It is also believed that he would materialize food items like fruits or sweets in front of the devotees. He also healed illnesses of devotees. He emphasized two key factors - Shraddha (faith) and Saburi (patience). Sai Baba always believed in one supreme deity and encouraged his followers to have faith in the Almighty.

Millions of people around the world are drawn to Shirdi Sai Baba due to his teachings of love, compassion, and universal brotherhood. His teachings resonated with people from all walks of life, regardless of their backgrounds or beliefs. Besides, Sai Baba had earned a reputation for performing miracles and answering devotees' prayers. He transcended religious boundaries, uniting people from all faiths under the banner of "सबका मालिक एक" (Sabka Malik Ek- meaning Everyone's God is One).

His message of faith, patience, and selfless service continues to inspire people, making him a beloved spiritual figure.

Thursday is considered particularly auspicious for worshipping Shirdi Sai Baba because it is dedicated to Gurus in Hindu tradition, and Sai Baba is revered as a Guru, or spiritual teacher. Specifically, Thursday is known as "Guruvar" in Sanskrit, further emphasizing its significance for guru worship. Today, Shirdi Sai Baba has hundreds of temples and millions of followers around the world. There is a surge of devotees on Thursdays at the Sai Baba temples.

Samadhi Location: Shirdi, a small rural town in the Rahata Taluka of Ahilyanagar district in the Mahārāshtra state of India. Shirdi is a secular place where all religions are treated as one. It is a major global pilgrimage site with extensive temple complex and facilities. Shree Saibaba Sansthan Trust, Shirdi, controls and manages the daily activities at the Shree Saibaba Samadhi Temple. It also provides various facilities like accommodation, food (Free for the poor), refreshments, and lot more.

The nearest airport is Shirdi international airport. Situated on the Ahmednagar-Manmad highway, you can also reach Shirdi from the new railway station at Sainagar. Manmad-Junction, Kopargaon and Nagarsul are other nearby railway stations on the Central Railway.

4. Gondavalekar Maharaj (Brahmachaitanya, 1845–1913)

Shri Brahmachaitanya Gondavalekar Maharaj was born in a small village called Gondavale, Mahārāshtra, India. His parents named him 'Ganapati.' He left home very early in his life, at the age of 12, in quest of spiritual guidance and Grace of a Guru to seek God. He finally found a Guru, "Shri Tukaram Chaitanya" (fondly called Shri Tukamai) from Yehlegaon. Tukamai initiated Maharaj into the mantra of Ram Naam.

Gondavalekar Maharaj was a lifelong devotee of Lord Rama and dedicated his life to spreading the mantra "Shri Ram Jai Ram Jai Jai Ram"

He lived a simple life, often conversing with people in simple language about worldly matters while also guiding spiritually knowledgeable individuals on the importance of chanting and Vedic mantras.

After extensive travel, he returned to promote bhakti through Ram naam japa, simplicity, and service. He preached surrender to the Divine Will through a 'Japam' of the Divine Name.

Samadhi Location: Gondavale, Satara district

5. Tembe Swami Maharaj (Shree Vasudevanand Saraswati, 1854–1914)

Tembe Swami Maharaj was born in 1854 in Mangaon, Maharashtra, and is believed to be an incarnation of Lord Dattatreya. He is known for his extensive travels across India, spreading spiritual knowledge and establishing numerous Dattatreya temples. He is also associated with the revival of certain sacred sites and the installation of Dattatreya idols.

A strict Vedic scholar and saint, he preached Advaita Vedanta, and upheld Sanatan Dharma.

He authored a significant body of literature, including works related to Dattatreya and spiritual teachings.

Tembe Swami Maharaj's teachings and his life of devotion continue to inspire many followers of Dattatreya and those seeking spiritual enlightenment.

He is credited with revealing the Mahamantra "Digambara Digambara Shripadha Vallabha Digambara" and popularized its chanting.

He is believed to have left his physical body at Garudeshwar, Gujarat, in 1914, at the age of 60.

Samadhi Location: Garudeshwar, Gujarat (though he lived extensively in Mahārāshtra).

Temples dedicated to him exist across Mahārāshtra.

6. Manik Prabhu Maharaj (1817–1865)

The great mystic saint and yogi Shri Manik Prabhu Maharaj (1817-1865) is hailed as the fourth incarnation of Lord Dattatreya and has an enormous following in the country. Shirdi Sai Baba, Shri Akkalkot Swami Maharaj, and Shri Gondavalekar Maharaj were Manik Prabhu's contemporaries, and they interacted with him on matters of deep spiritual wisdom.

Manik Prabhu's teaching, basically, lays stress on the path of Bhakti. His main teaching in Sanskrit was: एकं सत् विप्रा बहुधा वदन्ति (ekam sad vipra bahudha vadanti) meaning "Truth is one; the wise call it by many names."

Alongside his teachings, he moralized in the most remarkable manner on the Vedantic Truths concerning Spiritual Unity. He actively promoted interfaith harmony, especially among Hindus and Muslims.

He composed numerous bhajans, padas, stotras, shlokas, and ashtakas in Marathi, Kannada, Hindi, Urdu, Sanskrit, etc. His poetic legacy strengthened his message of devotion and unity.

In 1845, he established Maniknagar on the banks of the Viraja and Guruganga rivers near Humnabad (Bidar district, Karnataka). This became the hub for his spiritual vision, symbolized by an empty seat (gadi) inviting devotees to see the Supreme Reality in any form they worship. His spiritual lineage continues even today through the Shri Manik Prabhu Samsthan in Maniknagar, with celebrations like Datta Jayanti attracting thousands each year

His ashram is based near Bidar, close to the Mahārāshtra – Karnataka border.

Samadhi Location: Maniknagar (now in Karnataka, near Nanded)

Chapter - 19
Key Lessons

Many of the Mahāns of Mahārāshtra were not learned people. Some of them like Tukaram never went to school. Yet, they have inspired generations with their lives and teachings. Their wisdom continues to guide us toward living with joy, purpose, and compassion. Here's a summary of the key lessons they shared with all:

1. From Devotion to Liberation (Bhakti to Mukti)

The saints taught that deep love and devotion to God — Bhakti — is a powerful path to spiritual freedom (Mukti). They believed anyone, regardless of caste or status, could attain liberation through sincere devotion and surrender.

2. Equality for All

They strongly opposed caste-based discrimination and social injustice. To them, all people were equal in the eyes of God. Saints like Chokhamela, who came from marginalized communities, led by example and challenged the rigid social norms of their time.

3. Compassion and Service

Serving others was seen as a form of worship. The Mahāns emphasized kindness, empathy, and helping those in need. Sant Eknath's life of selfless service is a powerful example of this teaching.

4. Inner Purity and Simple Living

Rather than relying on rituals or outward displays of faith, the saints focused on inner purity — clean hearts and clear minds. They promoted simple, humble living and warned against greed and material excess.

5. Spiritual Wisdom for Everyone

To make their teachings accessible, the saints spoke and wrote in Marathi — the language of the people. This allowed everyone, not just the educated elite, to understand and follow the spiritual path.

6. Messages Through Music and Poetry

Their teachings were often shared through Abhangs — devotional poems and songs that were easy to understand and sing. Saints like Jnaneshwar translated sacred texts into Marathi, opening spiritual knowledge to all.

In essence, the Mahāns taught us to live with honesty, love, and simplicity. They encouraged a direct connection with the divine, promoted equality, and urged us to serve others with compassion.

Chapter - 20
Holy Places

This Punyabhoomi of Bharat (India) was not just a land covered with soil and mountains. It is a land where Mahāns were born generation after generation like the banana tree creating succeeding generations under its shelter. Many of them led humble lives and attained siddhi (salvation) at different times and places. Mahārāshtra has many such places where the saints are worshipped.

In this chapter, we provide some guidance on the places of worship and how to reach them. Maharashtrian saints are primarily worshipped at their respective temples and samadhis (tombs) throughout Mahārāshtra, with Pandharpur being a central pilgrimage site. Specifically, the shrines of Vithoba at Pandharpur, Dnyaneshwar at Alandi, and Tukaram at Dehu are major centers of worship. Additionally, the Sai Baba temple in Shirdi is a globally recognized pilgrimage site.

For the benefit of readers, we provide here a list of the prominent Mahārāshtrian saints' samādhi (final resting place) and worship sites, with names, locations, and travel guidance:

1. Alandi – Sant Dnyānēshwar

Alandi is famous as a pilgrimage town in Mahārāshtra, due to its association with the revered Marathi saint, Sant Dnyaneshwar. It's known as ***Devachi Alandi***, meaning "God's Alandi." The huge temple complex houses Sant Dnyaneshwar's samadhi (final resting place). The Indrayani River flows through Alandi and is considered sacred by the locals, with temples and other religious structures built along its bank. The town is also home to beautiful 13th-century temples, reflecting the rich religious and architectural heritage.

Location: Alandi, on the banks of the Indrayani River about 25 km north of Pune.

Site: Dnyānēshwar's Sanjeevan Samādhi Mandir under Siddheshwar temple complex in Bhosale Nagar

How to reach Alandi:

By road: Frequent buses, taxis, or car rides from Pune via NH 60 (about an hour)

By rail: Nearest main Railway station is Pune - from there, take a bus/taxi

By air: Nearest airport is Pune International (~30 kms)

2. Dehu – Sant Tukārām

Dehu holds immense importance as the place where Sant Tukaram was born and spent a significant part of his life. Tukaram, a prominent Varkari saint, is worshipped at his temple and samadhi in Dehu, near Pune.

There is a temple in Dehu dedicated to Sant Tukaram called Maharaj Gatha Mandir, Dehu. It is a modern building housing a big statue of Sant Tukaram. In the Gatha temple, about 4,000 Abhangs created by Tukaram maharaj are inscribed on the walls

Dehu also serves as a starting point for the annual Palkhi procession during the Hindu month of Ashadh, a major event for Tukaram's devotees.

Dehu also has a temple dedicated to Lord Vittal and his consort Rukmini, further enhancing its status as a pilgrimage site.

Saint Tukaram Vaikunthstan Temple is in Dehu. It is the spot from where Sant Tukaram ascended to Vaikunth in his mortal form. There is a nice ghat behind this temple with the Indrayani River flowing majestically through Dehu, adding to the town's religious and scenic appeal.

Location: Dehu village, Pune district (~10 km west of Alandi)

Site: Tukārām Maharaj's Samādhi Mandir and the nearby "Gāthā Mandir."

How to reach:

By road: Buses and taxis from Pune or Alandi.

By rail: From Dehuroad station or Pune Railway station, from there, take a bus/taxi

By air: Nearest airport is Pune International (~30 kms)

3. Paithan – Sant Eknāth

Location: Paithan, Aurangabad district, on the Godavari River (~100 km SE of Aurangabad)

Site: Eknāth's Jal-samādhi (watertomb) at Krishnakamalateerth with an adjacent temple

How to reach:

By rail: Paithan doesn't have a major station; best via Jalna or Aurangabad → taxi/bus.

By road: Regular buses connect it to Aurangabad and nearby cities.

4. Sajjangad – Sant Rāmdās

Location: Sajjangad Fort, Satara district (~20 km from Satara city)

Site: Samādhi of Sant Rāmdās (Guru of Shivaji Maharaj), atop the fort.

How to reach:

By road: Buses/taxis from Satara. Devotees may have to climb up part of the climb by foot.

5. Pandharpur – Sant Namdev (and many others)

Location: Pandharpur, Solapur district, on the Bhima River. This town in Solapur district is the most important pilgrimage site for the Varkari tradition, centered around the temple of Vithoba, a form of Krishna, and his consort Rakhumai. The annual Wari pilgrimage culminates here.

Site: Namdev's Samādhi in the Vittal-Rukmini Temple complex

How to reach:

By road/rail: Well-connected; special pilgrimage traffic during the Pandharpur Wari.

By pilgrimage: Palkhis depart from Alandi (Dnyaneshwar) and Dehu (Tukaram)

6. Shegaon – Sant Gajanan Maharaj

Location: Shegaon, Buldhana district, Vidarbha region

Site: Main Sansthan Temple built over his Samādhi (attained 1910)

How to reach:

By rail: Shegaon Railway Station (on Howrah–Nagpur–Mumbai line)

By road: Local buses or auto-rickshaws.

Major Pilgrimage Timings & Events

Ashādhi Ekādaśī (June–July):

Two Palkhi pilgrimages begin:

From Alandi for Dnyaneshwar (starting around June 19)

From Dehu for Tukārām (starting ~June 18)

Both converge in Pandharpur around July 5–6

Kārtiki Ekādaśī & saints' birth anniversaries: Marks annual congregations at Alandi, Dehu, Pandharpur, Sajjangad, etc.

Suggested Pilgrimage Route

Keep Pune as the base in Central Mahārāshtra.

Pune → Alandi (visit Dnyaneshwar Samādhi), Alandi → Dehu (visit Tukārām Samādhi)

Pune → Paithan (visit Eknāth's Samādhi)

Pune → Sajjangad (Rāmdās)

Pune → Pandharpur (Namdev + Wari culmination)

Pune → Shegaon (Gajanan Maharaj)

Chapter - 21
Resources for Information

Readers who wish to know more about the Mahāns of Mahārāshtra may like to visit the following places or institutions that provide lots of information related to the Mahāns of Mahārāshtra.

1. Sant Darshan Museum & Temple, Hadshi (Pune district)

It is a modern but richly curated museum featuring 1,200+ life-sized statues of saints including Sant Dnyaneshwar, Namdev, Tukaram, Eknath, etc. Integrated within a Vittal-Rukmini temple complex, it offers immersive storytelling through sculptures, murals, and audio-visual media. In this book, the author has included some pictures taken by him at this museum.

More information at the website https://santdarshanmuseum.com/.

2. Pandharpur & Vittal Temple Exhibitions

- The Pandharpur Varkari pilgrimage is not just restricted to devotion — it is a centuries-old living tradition, regularly documented through temple exhibitions and archives.
- The IGNCA Pandharpur Vari exhibition features the ceremonial processions (palkhis) of Sant Dnyaneshwar and Tukaram, curated by visual and material historians.
- The Vittal temple in Pune (Nana Peth) maintains statues of saints and carries historical records of the palkhi tradition, reflecting socio-religious continuity

3. **Deccan College Museum & Archives, Pune**

- Hosts ancient palm-leaf manuscripts and Modi-script documents from 17th-19th centuries.

- Includes rare copies of saint works, correspondence, and first-hand lineage records related to Tukaram and Dnyaneshwar.

Website: https://www.dcpune.ac.in/Museums.html

4. **Mumbai Marathi Grantha Sangrahalaya (MMGS)**

- Established in 1898, this is one of the oldest Marathi public libraries, recognized by the Mahārāshtra government as a "special museum." It has many rare documents.

- Houses hundreds of original saint writings, early printed Abhang collections, and hagiographies like *Bhaktavijaya* authored soon after these saints' lifetimes.

5. **Marathi Granth Sangrahalaya, Thane**

- Founded in 1893, this historic library holds rare old magazines and books that include saint poetry, commentaries, and early literary criticism — essential for research.

Website: https://granthyan.com/

6. **Bharat Itihas Sanshodhak Mandal, Pune**

- A major historical archive (100+ years), with about 1.5 million documents and manuscripts in Modi, Persian, Marathi, including bakhars (historic chronicles).

- Offers access to original texts from the era of saints like Namdev, Eknath, and Tukaram, crucial for dating and verifying biographies.

Website: https://rajwadehall.org/

Chapter - 22
Reference Books

There are many books, both in English and Marathi, that include references to the saints from Mahārāshtra. For the benefit of readers, we share a list of such books.

1. The Golden Age of India by Elphinstone
2. History of Hindu India by P.V. Kane
3. Musalmani Riyasat by Sardesai
4. Samartavatar by S.S. Dev
5. The Rise of Maratha Power by Justice M.G. Ranade
6. Mahārāshtra Saints by Rajwade
7. Sri Dasayana by Ananta Dass
8. Ramadas Bahar by Hanumant Swami
9. Dasavisramadham by Atmaram
10. Samartha Charitha by S.K. Altekar
11. Lectures by Swami Vivekananda
12. Samartha Che Samarthya by K.N. Athawale
13. Shivaji the Great by Dr. Balakrishna
14. Sri Ramadas Literature and work by N.R. Phatak
15. Chatrapati Shivaji by Kaluskar
16. Shahaji Bhonsle by Sardesai
17. Life of Eknath by S.B. Ranado and Panjarkar (book)
18. Shiva Bharat by Poet Paramananda

19. Shiv Sambhav by Khave Shastri

20. Vivek Sindhu by Mukunda Raj

21. Rama Sohala by Meru Swami

22. Bahamani Sultans by S.S. Dev

Apart from these, the Kumbakonam college library has some wonderful English books on the history of Shivaji written by the authors Yadhunath Sarcar, C.V. Vaidya and Majumdar.

Maha Bhakta vijaya is a Marathi text written by Mahipati around 1762 that extols the deeds of the saint-poets of the Varkari sect of Hinduism. The book contained stories about Maharashtrian saints and devotees of Pandarinath. It has been translated into various languages in India.

Other Publications of the Author

1. **The Glory of The Great Goddess in Lalitha Sahasranamam**

A Spiritual Exploration of the Thousand Names of the Goddess Lalitha based on

The Author's Lecture Series for the Sringeri Vidya Bharati Foundation (SVBF North), USA.

2. **SanGita - The Harmony of Sanskrit and the Gita**

A Primer on the Echoes of the Bhagavad Gita's Wisdom

These books are available through Amazon, Flipkart and many other outlets.

The Tamil Version of the book in Sr. No. 1 is under print. It is titled 'ஸ்ரீ லலிதா ஸஹஸ்ரநாமத்தில் லோகமாதாவின் மாஹாத்மியம்' and expected to be released in August 2025.

If you have any difficulty in procuring these books, please contact the author at gurujisubi@gmail.com

The author's spiritual videos: You may view the author's numerous videos on YouTube @Subi654.

While every effort has been made to ensure the accuracy of this book, some errors may have gone unnoticed. If you come across any inaccuracies or have suggestions for improvement, please don't hesitate to reach out. Your feedback is invaluable and will help enhance future editions. Contact E-mail: gurujisubi@gmail.com.

Thank you for your understanding and support!